UNLOCK

The Secret World Of Teenagers

Yaakov Y. Rosenthal

Motivational Press
LEADERS IN GLOBAL PUBLISHING

Unlock: The Secret World of Teenagers

Published by Motivational Press, Inc.
7777 N. Wickham Road, #12-247
Melbourne, FL 32940
www.MotivationalPress.com

Copyright 2014 © by Yaakov Y. Rosenthal
www.understandyourteenager.com

Cover design by Kaye Homecillo
Front cover photograph by Rosenthal Photo, Brooklyn, New York

All Rights Reserved

No part of this book may be reproduced or transmitted in any form by any means: graphic, electronic, or mechanical, including photocopying, recording, taping or by any information storage or retrieval system without permission, in writing, from the authors, except for the inclusion of brief quotations in a review, article, book, or academic paper. The authors and publisher of this book and the associated materials have used their best efforts in preparing this material. The authors and publisher make no representations or warranties with respect to accuracy, applicability, fitness or completeness of the contents of this material. They disclaim any warranties expressed or implied, merchantability, or fitness for any particular purpose. The authors and publisher shall in no event be held liable for any loss or other damages, including but not limited to special, incidental, consequential, or other damages. If you have any questions or concerns, the advice of a competent professional should be sought.

Manufactured in the United States of America.

ISBN: 978-1-62865-061-7

Contents

Dedication 5
Acknowledgements 7
Handwriting analysis? Do you really believe that's a science? 9
Foreword 11
Autobiography in Five Short Chapters 13
Introduction 15

Chapter One: My beginnings 17
Chapter Two: What Is Handwriting Analysis? 22
Chapter Three: Margins: The Personal Bubble 26
Chapter Four: The Roller Coaster 34
Chapter Five: The Big Blob: Concealing Mistakes 38
Chapter Six: Our Energy Source 43
Chapter Seven: Information Versus Action 50
Chapter Eight: In the I's 58
Chapter Nine: Combo of Champions: Competence and Compassion 67
Chapter Ten: Guiding Principles 71
Chapter Eleven: Putting It All Together 83
Chapter Twelve: OWE to BFF 89
Chapter Thirteen: Abuse: The Life Changer 97
Chapter Fourteen: Understanding Is the Key 105
Epilogue: I Wish 109

About the Author 111
Appendix A 112
Appendix B 113

Unlock: The Secret World of Teenagers

Dedication

To my precious grandchildren who will, G-d willing, grow up and thrive in a more compassionate world.

Acknowledgements

To the Lubavitcher Rebbe for helping me realize the value of my life, and to G-d for life itself.

To my wife: I married you for many, many, many reasons, but your ability to compose a sentence and spell became an extra bonus. I love you.

To my late mother and father of blessed memory, who would "help" me write my school papers, always had faith in me and loved me to wholeness.

To my sister Amy, for being a top-notch sounding board and a good example to follow.

To my children and their spouses: to Goldie, Menucha, Yossie, Chavie, Nuchie, Avremi, Chayale, and Riki for their encouragement, support, and proofreading.

Special thanks to Nuchie Schapiro, whose time and concern for this project were instrumental in helping me develop it.

To Rabbi Sholom Ciment, Rabbi Moshe Lieblich, Rabbi Uri Perlman, Mrs. Dina Gorkin and Mrs. Hinda Leah Scharfstein who challenged me, guided me, and stood by me.

To Ann McIndoo, my author's coach, who got this book out of my head and into your hands. Without Ann's beautiful system, my sixth attempt to write a book would be lost on my computer with the other five. I cannot thank you enough.

To Shana Guzick, for all of your help that allowed this book to mature into a final product. You are like a cellophane artist, preserving my voice and making the book flow.

To elane.com, all the graphic artists, and especially Kaye Homecillo for her wonderful cover design.

To all the beautiful teenagers I have met along the journey who have taught me so much about life and how beautiful, precious, and fragile it is.

And to me, for writing a book. Imagine, I did it. It's truly amazing.

I am grateful to you all.

Handwriting Analysis: Do You Really Believe That's a Science?

by Dena Gorkin
Principal, Bnos Chomesh Academy

That was the reaction of one of the judges as he viewed my exhibit at the science fair. I was in the eleventh grade. I was surprised at the comment, even a bit insulted. But it had an effect; it made me more interested than ever before in the science—yes, science—of graphology.

It is a fascinating area of study. But, like in medicine, it's not only about the science; it's about the practitioner, as well. And my school, Bnos Chomesh Academy, has been blessed with a marvelous practitioner of graphology. When Yaakov Rosenthal first started working with my students, I was excited because I felt that his sessions would add a dimension of fun to our curriculum. The students would think it was cool that he could see some of their traits in their handwriting. What I did not anticipate was the incisive manner in which Mr. Rosenthal would see into our students' souls and help them to grow in ways I could never have expected.

When we encounter a student who presents as a brick wall, it is difficult for us to figure out what is going on and what approach to take with her. With all the patience our teachers can muster, we sometimes find ourselves stumped for a strategy. Enter Yaakov Rosenthal's special brand of therapy, and a girl whom we have been struggling to reach for six months is talking after 45 minutes. When I look at a student and talk to her about her behavior, she goes on the defensive. When Mr. Rosenthal looks at her handwriting and says to her, "You are telling me here that you don't trust people," it just breaks down barriers. She can't argue with the assertion because she herself told it to him, indisputably, right there on paper. The work on personal growth can start immediately because he has cut through all the layers of denial.

I should mention that it is not just Mr. Rosenthal's skill that makes his magic work. Mr. Rosenthal brings to his work not only years of experience but also his characteristic warmth and caring. The combination is stunning. The young people he works with are given more than insight into their behavior; they are also given gentle guidance towards a more positive way of leading their lives. They feel that he is a safe person to talk to and know that they will get the encouragement they need if they share information that makes them feel vulnerable. They will never be judged.

Many times throughout the year, students have stopped me to ask, "When is Mr. Handwriting Guy coming?" or "Can you get Mr. Rosenthal this week?" When they ask that, I realize that they are either stuck at some difficult juncture and need him to help them work their way through it, or they have made some important strides and want to share their accomplishments with him. Either way, it is an incredible blessing for us to have him as part of our educational support team here at Bnos Chomesh.

I am thrilled that Yaakov Rosenthal has decided to share his gift with the world in the form of this book. It is my fervent hope that with Mr. Rosenthal's guidance, parents, educators, and youth directors of all kinds will be able to improve their understanding of the children and teens in their care. With greater understanding, we can usher the adults of tomorrow into adulthood with more self-awareness, more confidence, and greater ability to be productive members of our society.

Dena Horwin

Foreword

Sam, a fourteen-year-old student, came to me one day very upset. He and his father had always had a great relationship. Recently, though, Sam had started feeling that his father just didn't "get" him, and that, for some reason, their father-son relationship wasn't working at all.

I asked Sam whether his father had been treating him differently, or if he'd seen any changes in his father's behavior, but Sam shook his head "no." He said his father was constantly praising him and was always there to support him; in fact, his father showed no signs of negativity towards him whatsoever. But inside, Sam confided, he was experiencing some seriously confusing turmoil, and that feeling was bleeding into everything—including his relationship with his none-the-wiser father.

Sam was hoping I would speak to his father about this sudden shift, but I told him that his father wasn't the one who needed to be clued in…Sam was. He needed strengthening from the inside. By using his handwriting to uncover intimate details about his thoughts, feelings, and struggles, I was able to give Sam a deeper look into his true self and the changes he was experiencing. This set him on the road to rebuilding his relationship with his father—and himself—from the inside out.

Unlock: The Secret World of Teenagers offers a unique approach to help parents, educators, and teens themselves to better understand teenagers' inner workings. Using handwriting to turn frustration into compassion and bewilderment into competence, the pages that follow will allow you to see the truth behind what you think you already know about your teens, while creating space for them to develop self-respect, introspection, communication, and trust.

The purpose of this book is not to teach the entire body of graphology, handwriting analysis, but simply to provide some of the tools that handwriting experts use to foster positive growth within teens.

Unlock will help you identify handwriting indicators that are particularly associated with the uniqueness of teenagers, as well as understand principles that relate to teenagers' growth into adulthood, seeking to clarify the confusions, fears, and angers that so many teens share. When teens and those around them learn that *most* things that teens do are *completely normal,* everyone gains hope and can begin to move in the most positive direction.

Let us begin.

Autobiography in Five Short Chapters

By Portia Nelson

I.

I walk down the street.
There is a deep hole in the sidewalk.
I fall in.
I am lost... I am hopeless.
It isn't my fault.
It takes forever to find a way out.

II.

I walk down this same street.
There is a deep hole in the sidewalk.
I pretend I don't see it.
I fall in again.
I can't believe I am in the same place.
But, it isn't my fault.
It still takes a long time to get out.

III.

I walk down the same street.
There is a deep hole in the sidewalk.

I see it is there.

I still fall in… it's a habit.

My eyes are open.

I know where I am.

It's my fault.

I get out immediately

IV.

I walk down the same street.

There's a deep hole in the sidewalk.

I walk around it.

V.

I walk down another street.

Introduction

There is a profound emotional difference between a nine-year-old and a 13-year-old. Nine-year-olds have a simple way of looking at the world. Their biggest dilemma is choosing which seat they want in the car. Their most crucial life decision is which backpack to wear. Their greatest joy is a sleepover. Their greatest disappointment is broccoli. Their lives are not complicated and, as a result, neither are the lives of their caregivers. Okay, they might argue when it's bedtime, but overall, these young children are just plain cute.

Suddenly, though, at age twelve or thirteen, these cuties have monsters implanted within them. They start categorizing people: girls and boys, old and young, cool and annoying. They are opposed to just about everything. They're argumentative. They don't like to wake up, but they don't like to go to bed, either. Though they're not very sure of themselves on the inside, they do their best to hide that from the world. They may not be confident, but they certainly know what they don't want: authority. They don't like family rules. Nothing gives them more pleasure than when their parents aren't around. They do not enjoy being controlled. Consequences completely irrelevant to their reality, they think they can handle it all. Although they desire to take care of themselves (and believe—*know*—that they are capable), they have not developed the tools to do so.

This book has a twofold agenda: one, to give patience and hope to parents and teachers of young teenagers,[1] and two, to give teenagers an

---

1 *While much of the information in this book is relevant to people of all ages, the content herein is intended to focus primarily on younger teenagers, since older teenagers are already becoming more adult-like and often do not fall into the same maturity category as younger teenagers.*

understanding of what they're going through. We will focus on effectively communicating to teenagers what the tools for independence are in a way that the teens can really receive the information. This book is not about telling teens what they have to do; rather, it is about telling you, the reader, how to suggest and motivate. Change happens through many series of nudges, of minute, almost immeasurable steps. Rarely do we see great change happen instantly.

Graphology is the study of handwriting as used to gather information about a person's personality. Throughout my career as a graphologist, I've identified several unique components to a teenager's handwriting. I hope and pray that this book will be a meaningful beginning to open your mind, heart, and understanding of this essential growth that occurs between the ages of twelve and twenty. During these years, nearly every person will undergo a transformation from being totally unfamiliar with the effects of his actions, to being an adult who can make conscious choices to integrate, destroy, or improve his or her world.

This book is not going to turn you into a graphologist, nor is this the last book that needs to be written on the subject. However, once you know some key details—the challenges and fears of every teen—you will be able to look at teens with more compassion, and, as a result, they will then see you as being more understanding (and they'll be right!).

When you achieve compassion by having true empathy for their suffering, confusion, joy, and contentment, you will then become someone in their lives whom they can rely upon to "get" them. This in itself is very comforting for an emotional teenager. Then, you can achieve competence when, as a caregiver, you impart wisdom to effect positive change and push away some darkness, which will allow a bit of normalcy into a teenager's life. Once you have these two ingredients, compassion and competence, you will begin to develop trust.

Chapter One

My Beginnings

In 1988, I became a certified graphologist under the guidance of the late Felix Klein. Known as the "Dean of American Graphology," he towered over the field until his passing in 1994. His resumé alone is testament to his excellence, having worked for the United Nations, ATT, the State of New York, and a number of prominent universities. He was one of the world's top-ranked document examiners and testified in hundreds of court cases, many political in nature. He was the founder and president of the National Bureau of Document Examiners, as well as a president of the American Association of Handwriting Analysts. Simply put, he was the best.

Resumé aside, I was most impressed with his ability to attach graphology to psychology and human nature. Unlike other graphologists who simply stated the facts about the subject's handwriting and left the subject to apply the information on his own, to Felix Klein, graphology was a tool to help map out a person's individual path to growth. Where a "regular" graphologist would tell someone, "your handwriting shows that you're uptight," Felix Klein would tell him why this was the case and what he could do about it.

It was in those early days under his tutelage that I chose to use this personal approach in my own graphology work. Since then, I have had thousands of individual sessions and given hundreds of lectures all over the world. I have worked with private detectives, social workers, and psychologists, and have been a popular speaker at bookstores, gala dinners, and even religious group events. But no job had an impact on me quite like one particular lecture in 1998.

I had been invited to speak about graphology to a group of about 60 high school students. The topic was "Finding You in Your Handwriting." I discussed the concept that when a person thinks a thought and puts it on paper, what creates the words is not just his muscles or nerves but also a certain force, the force that keeps the person alive and, upon leaving the body, causes the person to pass away despite the fact that those muscles and nerves are still intact.

After my 45-minute talk, a question and answer session, and a few semi- private meetings with a handful of students, I was ready to leave. But there was one last person who wanted to talk to me. His name was Tom.[2] The 22-year-old assistant teacher approached me with his handwriting sample and requested a quick analysis. I didn't know it at the time, but this small encounter would drastically change the focus of my career.

He was about six feet tall, thin, and confident. His students were afraid of him. He did not seem overly impressed with my presentation or abilities. He had a tough, "I don't believe this stuff" demeanor, and began engaging in what I call "Stump the Graphologist." I had played the game before.

His handwriting was small and clearly written with creative strokes. He filled the page with writing, leaving a well-balanced margin all around. His words were comfortably spaced and he pressed hard on the paper. His sample showed that he was very organized, clear thinking, detail oriented, and an information-based thinker. As he told me later, he was somewhat impressed by hearing these details, but only a little. He still felt my report was too general. I then told him about his need to watch a situation before he acted. I explained to him that he paced himself so his energy would last throughout a long day. I told him that he was very untrusting in new situations and was intimidated by others who seemed to know more than he did. Last, I told him that he was very soft hearted

and sensitive, that he had created a hard exterior in order to protect this sensitivity, that he exhibited a "don't mess with me, you can't hurt me" attitude, but that underneath this front was a very sensitive, caring, soft person. Hearing this last bit, his jaw dropped; his attitude toward graphology had changed.

Fast forward six years to 2004. Tom had become the principal of a small private high school. Soon after he accepted the position, he asked me to join his staff as a part-time counselor for his students. He believed my work to be insightful and helpful. Since then, my work has taken on a specialty focus with teens. Coupled with my graphology, I have been working with teenagers for the past nine years as a certified counselor and life coach, joining the staffs of several schools and summer camps.

With the help of graphology, this book will help educators, parents, and teens themselves to identify normal teenage behavior. Teenagers really don't know what's normal and what's not. They know cause and effect, they know what parents complain about, what teachers reward them for, what's expected of them. But they are putting those pieces together and just beginning to figure out what's good, what's bad, who they are as individuals. Most are just teenagers doing teenage things. Most just need a listening friend, a kind word, or an understanding adult. Most need a cheerleader rooting them on. And the job of parents and teachers is to fill that role, guiding teenagers and helping them each discover their personal uniqueness within society.

---

2   *All names have been changed.*

Notes

Chapter Two

What Is Handwriting Analysis?

We were all taught as young children how to write, the basics of how to form the letters and then how to spell words. No matter the language, in those early days, the conscious mind was totally in control of our writing. When we carefully drew an A and a P and a P and an L and an E, we had to think about exactly how to create each letter and how to combine those letters to spell a whole word: apple.

Through practice, writing became more automatic until there was really very little—if any—conscious thought involved whatsoever. Having reached that point, we're no longer thinking about the structure of each letter or the combination of letters that create a word; we're simply communicating an idea onto the page. We get to a point where we think a thought and instinctively start to write. What moves the hand to create the writing is not the conscious mind but the person's enlivening energy, life force, soul, personality, or whatever else you want to call it.

This force, unique to each person, is the reason that, even though we Americans are all taught the same Palmer Method to learn "correct" penmanship, Sally's handwriting always looks like the queen's, and Matt's always looks like chicken scratch. (By the way, Chicken Scratch Guy might not be just too dumb to write properly; he might simply not care to communicate to others, or he might even be so bright that his hand cannot keep up with his brain's speed.) By the time a child becomes a teenager, he usually already has his own handwriting, with its individual shortcuts and personal flares. Most students don't write like the Palmer Method once they become teenagers. (And for those who *do* continue to write with such precision into their teenage and adult years, still taking the time to form the letters as their teachers practiced with them, graphology shows that these people are amazing rule followers. Because of this unique personality trait, these individuals are perfect candidates to become executive secretaries, policemen, and teachers.)

When a person passes away, his body is still intact, but his hands are not moving, his eyes can't see, and his ears can't hear. Something has left the body. It is this force that allowed the person to move, think, talk, act, see, hear...in a way that was uniquely *him*. This same force allowed him to move his hand in a way that transcribed his thoughts into words on paper, also in a way that was uniquely him. When he wrote, it wasn't just his finger that approached the paper; it was *him*. He wrote the words as only *he* could write the words.

Most people are completely unaware that their personalities are visible in their handwriting. They go their entire lives being confused about so many things within themselves, all the while not knowing that they have an indispensable tool at their disposal.

There are twenty major indicators (see Appendix A) that allow a graphologist to analyze a person's handwriting, such as where the writer begins writing on the page, the size of the writer's margins, and how close to each other the writer's letters and words are. Most people think neatness is *the* indicator, not knowing that it is only one of twenty. Each indicator means something on its own, but by combining them together, a three-dimensional personality presents itself.

While, of course, every person's thoughts and challenges are unique, there are definitely major patterns. With regard to teenagers in particular, having analyzed handwriting samples from hundreds of teens and coached many of these teens, as well, I have discovered certain themes that are central to this specific period of growth in their lives, as well as handwriting indicators that help gauge where a teen is in that process. Of the twenty general indicators, I've isolated a few that are most useful in analyzing a teenager's handwriting.

Most teens are going through similar challenges. These six handwriting indicators will allow you to see what those challenges are, and what the teen needs in order to work through them.

Notes

Chapter Three

Margins: The Personal Bubble

Whhen a writer approaches a blank piece of paper, he will start writing wherever he feels comfortable. The upper margin and left margin are created by the beginning strokes of the writer.

The right margin is created when the writer decides to end a line and start the next one. An average margin (Figure 3-1) is about an inch on each side of a standard 8.5"x11" page. (This is the paper size used for all graphology measurements in this book, though some samples have been cut or resized here for formatting purposes.) The upper margin is usually slightly larger than the side margins.

Margins are our comfort zone; they show how we feel about life, other people, new things and old things, how we deal with the outside environment, and how we try to control its effects on us. Accordingly, margins also show our defense mechanisms.

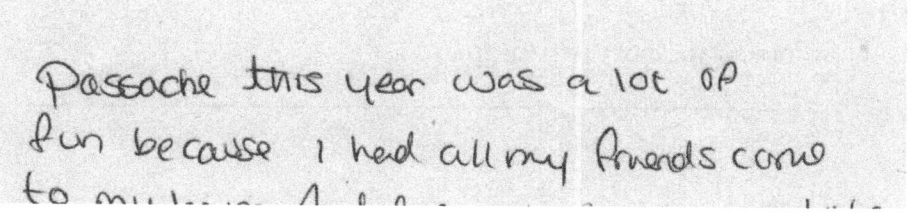

Figure 3-1

Upper Margins

The upper margin reflects the writer's attitude toward others. The larger the margin, the more respect the writer has for authority, and vice versa. Let's look at two samples that have almost no upper margin (Figure 3-2).

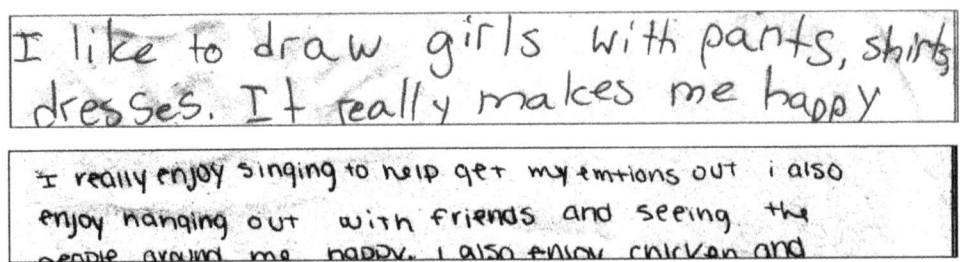

Figure 3-2

As represented by their nearly nonexistent upper margins, these two teenagers have a hard time respecting others, especially authority figures. They have got a bit of an attitude. They're a little angry, have a wall up and aren't going to respect you unless you have done something to deserve it. The space at the top of a page is a respectful space; it allows the words on the page to be read more easily. When a person invades this margin space by neglecting to form a proper upper margin, it means he's not in the habit of respecting others so quickly. When you meet these two teens, you are not going to find them to be overly friendly, nice, or helpful. They are both a little cautious about opening up to someone who hasn't yet earned it.

Now look at the next two samples.

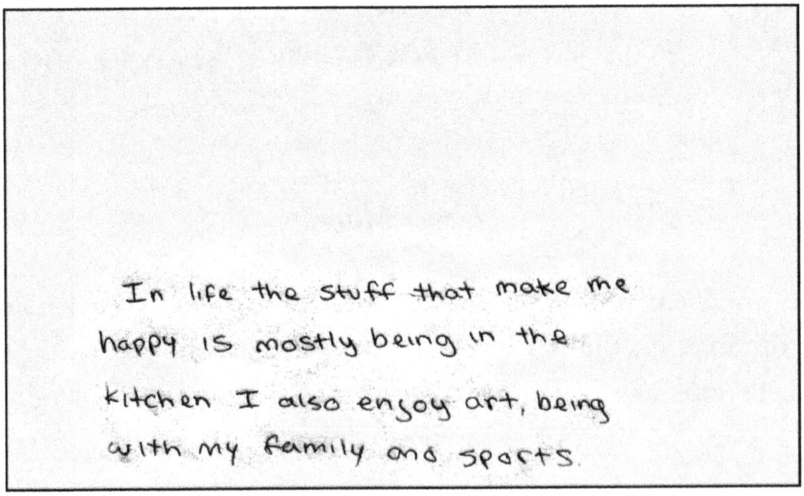

Figure 3-3

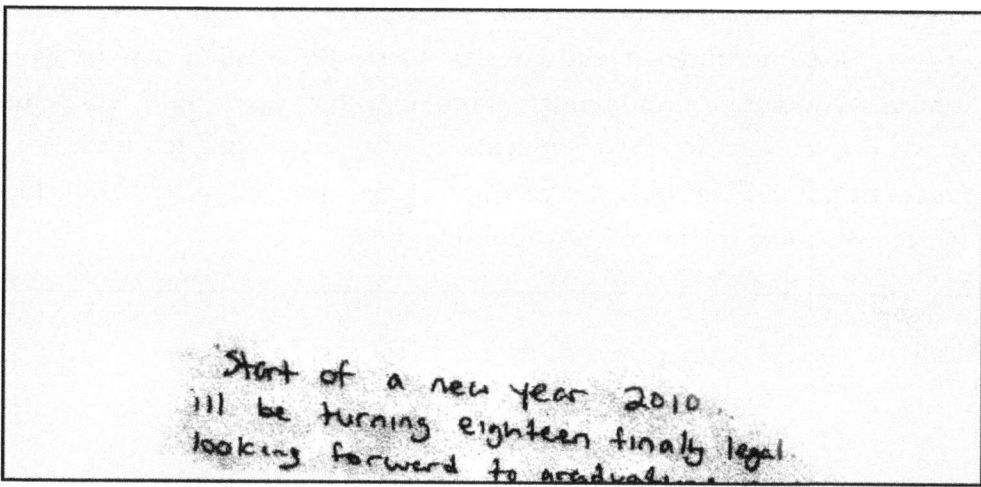

Figure 3-4

The upper margins are large; the writers have both started writing far down. There is a large space between the beginning of the writing and the upper edge of the paper, indicating writers with strong defense mechanisms. Unlike the writers who use the paper starting all the way from the very top, these teens are so sweet, so respectful, so nice, so friendly, and seemingly so open. But underneath this warmth, they are defensive; they are analytical people, "thinkers" who don't quickly accept other people. These teenagers have that by projecting a friendly, happy outward appearance, they will be able to take the time to determine whether they would like to join in with, accept, trust, or learn from a new person. While writers who start at the top of the paper prefer to actually display this distrust before accepting others, our big top margin writers put on a happy face and a friendly show. This gives them the chance to decide whether they want this person in their lives without burning bridges while they think it over.

Left Margin

A large left margin represents a person who doesn't like to deal with the past; he prefers to avoid the pain, frustration, and insecurity that the past brings. He doesn't want to see or believe that he is in any way defined by his past so he buries it and constantly tries to create a new present. Sometimes there's a deep hidden pain; in other cases, this represents unremarkable, regular, classic insecurities. But watch out for these; the pattern of not dealing with the past is a pattern that often begins during the teen years and carries on into adult life (Figure 3-5).

Start of a new year 2010.
ill be turning eighteen finaly legal.
looking forward to graduation highschool.
and looking forward to my brothers

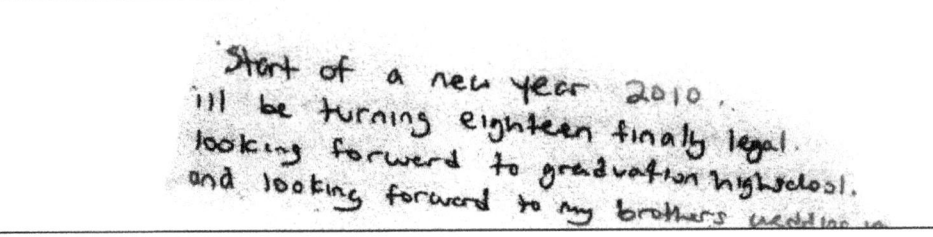

Figure 3-5

Right Margin

The right margin represents the future. Those who make large right margin are afraid to travel into new areas, unfamiliar territory, places where they're not proficient. These writers like to stay in their comfort zones. They may be very bright, but they don't like to show that there's something they don't know. Wary of new situations, these writers probably won't be the ones to volunteer for something they have never done (Figure 3-6).

I love being outside, hiking, swimming, dancing
in the rain. Being around the people I love makes

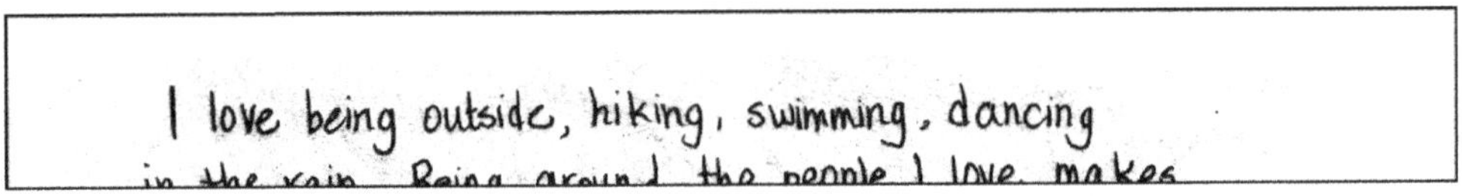

Figure 3-6

Combination

A page with no margins at all around (top and both sides) shows someone who likes to save things. This person begins writing from the tippy top and goes from edge to edge; he doesn't want to waste one single piece of space on the page (Figure 3-7).

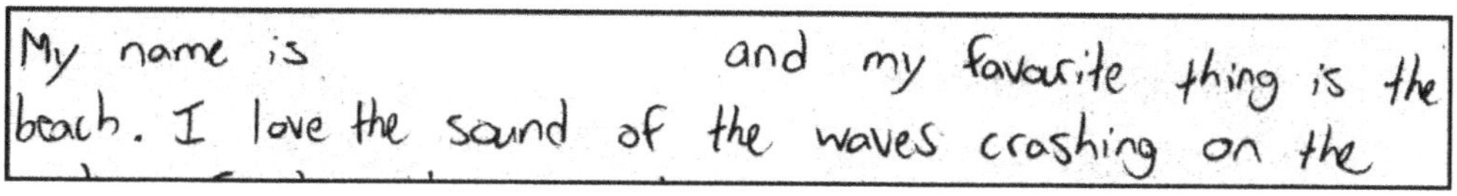

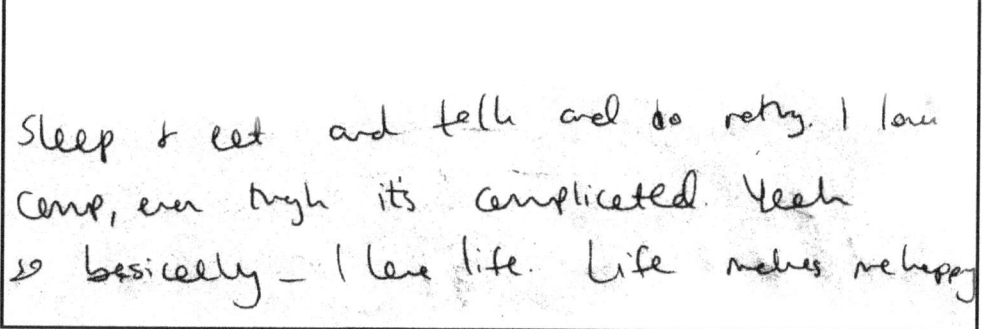

Figure 3-7

Figure 3-8

In the case of a teenager (unlike developed adults), lack of margins may not necessarily mean the writer likes to hold onto things. These teenaged edge-to-edge writers may likely be people who have no space for other people's information. They know it all and are very difficult to tell anything to. This is typically just another defense mechanism. Additionally, there is a big chance that they don't respect other people and don't want others to tell them what to do. These teenagers may be difficult students, with the exception for one or two teachers who break through to them, and who the students think are cool. Even if they write edge-to-edge with an upper margin (Figure 3-8), opening up to the potential of learning from someone else, trusting is difficult. They'd rather not show vulnerability.

Look at Figure 3-9. Now that you know all about margins, what does Figure 3-1 tell you?

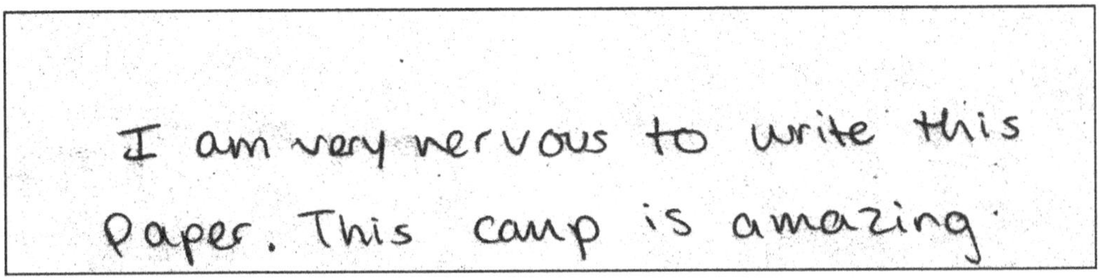

> I am very nervous to write this paper. This camp is amazing.

Figure 3-9

The example above reflects a teenager who is comfortable with herself. Upper margins show the teen is respectful of others. She's happy, she feels at ease with who she is, and she's not intimidated by interpersonal interactions. Her side margins are in good proportion to the size of her upper margin. She takes lessons from the past (left margin), and is willing to try new things that she's never done before (right margin). She is comfortable in her environment. She is and she's okay with that.

Keep in mind that her balanced margins do *not* make her a better person; they only make her... her. There's no right or wrong here.

Notes

Chapter Four

The Roller Coaster

When we start writing from the left and move to the right on unlined paper, the challenge is to keep the line horizontally straight. Many teenagers write in lines that look a bit like roller coasters: wavy, with the words traveling up and down, up and down (Figure 4-1).

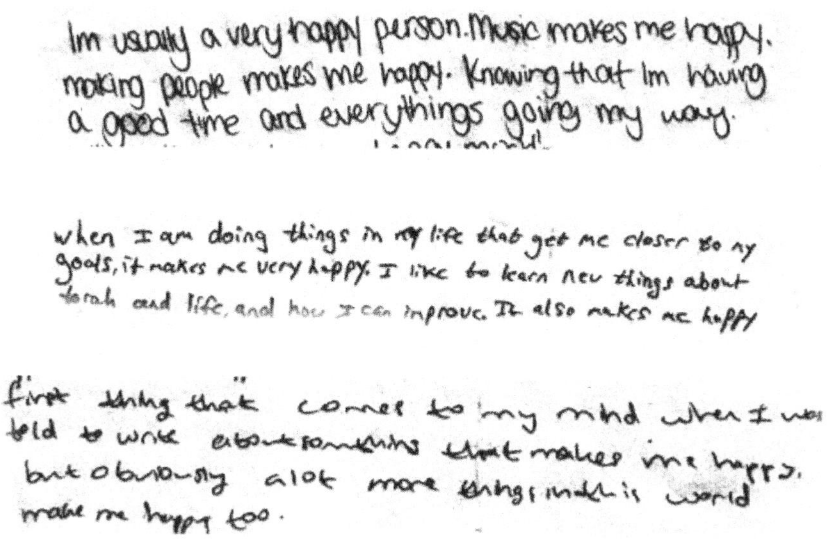

Figure 4-1

Each sample above shows the wavy movement of roller coaster lines. The sizes of the letters and spacing are irrelevant; the wavy movement is obvious. On a simple level, this roller coaster movement expresses unsettledness. The upward movement (positive, confident) takes a turn and goes down (unsure, worried). Then, confidence comes back again. *I feel good about myself. No, no I don't. Well, maybe I feel okay about myself. Eh, no, I really don't! ...Or do I?*

In a teenager's handwriting, it gets a bit more specific; this roller coaster writing, for teens, usually indicates their desire for—and simultaneous fear of—increased control of self. They lack the life experience necessary to develop any true sense of confidence in decision-making, but, at the same time, they're becoming aware of both their individuality and their capacity to do. The ups are realizing they have power; the downs are the fear that comes with realizing their experience doesn't correspond with their feelings of what they think they might just possibly be potentially somewhat capable of...maybe. *Who am I? Where am I going? What am I? How do I differ from my parents? What do I need them to do for me? What can I do on my own? Where is my control?* It's exhausting!

Rules are the opposite of independence. A rule makes them dependent and they don't like it. Curfews, homework, chores... these strip teenagers of their ability to do exactly what they want. Their lives become exhausting, tiring, frustrating, annoying. Every adult seems to stand in their way. *I don't know what exactly* me *is, but I'm going to be me; I want to be me!* And so, they feel confident one moment and insecure the next. They feel a sense of control of their destiny, and then, at the next moment they feel utterly squashed. They don't realize or care that rules are how parents keep children safe while they learn to be... drumroll... independent!

This transition can be made a bit smoother if parents and educators communicate to the teens that *nobody* is entirely independent. (See "Independence Is in the Eye of the Beholder" in Chapter 10.)

Roller coaster lines will disappear when teens feel secure with themselves and their direction in life and at peace with the amount of control they can exert.

Notes

Chapter Five

The Big Blob: Concealing Mistakes

Unlock: The Secret World of Teenagers

Ever look at a page and the first thing that jumps at you is a big ink blob?

I enjoy talking with friends and family.
I enjoy seeing a project to the end.

Dance every time I hear it. My heart lifts every time I hear the music. the music lifts me up. It could be anything I won't go past my limits in lifting weights and stuff like that. It makes you more stable mentally and physically.

What makes me happy is when im home and I can just chill with my family and friends. I am happy when I go moun

Figure 5-1

Look at this ink blob; it actually looks like the state of New York. Under this blob is a mistake. The person wrote something, realized it was a mistake, and didn't want anybody to see. Hence, a blob was born.

The funny thing, though, is that when you look at these four examples, the first thing to jump out at you are the blobs. They each shout, "I just made a mistake. It's underneath this blob here. Wanna see it?"

Mistakes help us grow. They are learning opportunities. But, for whatever reason, teenagers have somehow learned that those mistakes put them in a negative light. They have a false belief that if they cover over the mistake, no one will know that they made one. Easier, quicker, is to draw a simple line through something you don't want someone to read and then follow it by the right piece of information. This is the healthy way to correct a mistake. A person subconsciously accepts a crossed-out line as one not to be read, moving right along to the next word. No big deal. Who cares. But when a reader comes to a big blob, he wonders, *I wonder what's under there.... Must be something really bad!*

Imagine two parents sitting at the kitchen table. In walks their three-year-old daughter Becky, who, facing the wall, is careful not to come anywhere close to looking at her parents. Her parents, of course, watch her as she comes in, tiptoes to the refrigerator, opens it, and takes out the remnants of last night's chocolate cake. She closes the refrigerator, never looking into the room, always facing the wall, and leaves, cake in hand. This little girl is certain that her parents did not see her, since she did not see her parents. Like the blob people, since she did her very best to hide her cake misdeed, she thinks nobody will ever know. Meanwhile, her bizarre (albeit not bizarre for a three-year-old) behavior makes her onlookers pay even closer attention.

Teenagers need to be gently reminded that there's no need—or help— in covering up mistakes. A person isn't defined by his misspelled word, financial mishap or wrecked car. Rather, we are defined by how we handle the situation. There's nothing wrong with making mistakes. And, if we put in the effort to right our wrongs, our mistakes can become our most positive, powerful moments in life.

Notes

Chapter Six

Our Energy Source

Human beings run on energy. We need food, water, sunlight, and sleep to keep us going. In addition to our physical energy sources, our social interactions can either energize or deplete us.

On a basic level, people energize themselves in one of two ways: connecting or disconnecting. I'm not talking about whether a person is social or introverted. This is about whether a person needs to do with the person's social interactions being good or poor. It's about whether a person needs to go inward or outward to recharge.

A few years ago, a mother came to me and said she was concerned about her daughter Allie. The woman was divorced and worried that she'd messed Allie up. All Allie would do after school was go into her bedroom and read. Allie was friendly; she had no problems with friends at school, but when she came home, she was a reader. Allies' mother, on the other hand, was a real communicator; she was a real estate agent, loved to be around people, loved to talk, and loved to connect. She brought Allie's handwriting—along with Allie—because she wanted Allie to hear that there was something wrong with going into her room to read alone.

It was obvious that the mother's mode of keeping energized was through connecting with others. But Allie needed the exact opposite; she craved me- time. As I told the mother and daughter this, Allie pumped her fist *Yessss!*" while the mother's jaw dropped. Obviously, once the mother understood the concept of social energy, she understood her daughter much better.

The Connector

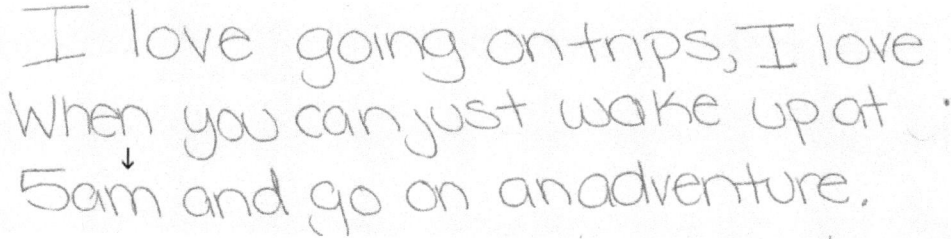

Figure 6-1

Some people need to be very social, need to connect, need to be in a relationship (Figure 6-1). Relationships enliven them and make them feel good. If someone would send such a person on a free week-long vacation on a mountaintop surrounded by nature and books, but without a cell phone, telephone or internet, he would return home utterly exhausted. These people lose energy when they're not around people and gain it when they connect with others.

In handwriting, when the spaces between a person's words are roughly the size of their letter M, the person's needs for space versus interaction are very balanced. In Figure 6-1, notice the closeness of the words to each other. Now find the letter M in "5 a.m." The M is larger than the space between the words. The words are like people. They're close to each other; the writer likes to keep people close, to be in the physical presence of others. For this person, a cruise would be a perfect way to vacation and refresh; seven days of all the interaction a person could want.

Me-Timer

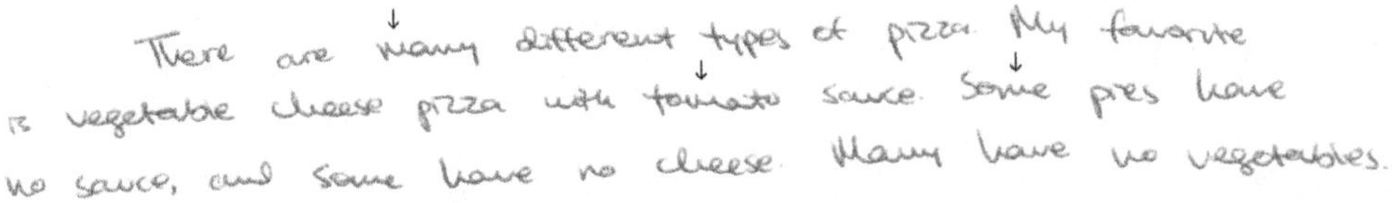

> *There are many different types of pizza. My favorite is vegetable cheese pizza with tomato sauce. Some pies have no sauce, and some have no cheese. Many have no vegetables.*

Figure 6-2

Now look at Figure 6-2. This person needs space, needs some distance, needs time by himself, me-time. Offer him a vacation on a cruise liner, where all of the activities—discos, massage parlors, ping pong, swimming, and eating—involve relating with other people and doing things with them, and he will come back exhausted, needing some time by himself to re-energize.

Look at the distance between the words in Figure 6-2. Find the letter M in the word "many" (first line, third word). The letter M is smaller than the space between the words. This doesn't mean that the writer is antisocial or socially awkward. On the contrary, he could very well be quite socially savvy but simply need me-time to re-energize. Interacting may be fun for him, but too much of it comes at the cost of depleting his energy. Me-time is a gift he gives himself. For this person, a week on a mountaintop sounds very inviting.

Two lessons come from understanding the differences between connectors and me-timers. Firstly, it is important that teenagers and their parents appreciate their own personal needs. Their desires to energize and satisfy themselves are specific, unique, personalized, and good. There is a comfort in knowing "I need this, and I am respecting myself by giving it to myself." Secondly, this understanding is of great help in relating to others. It's very common for a social person who needs to connect to be a little put off by someone who needs me-time, like the teenager who calls his friend and says, "Let's do something!" only to hear his buddy respond, "I'm reading right now, I can't come." The connector can't depend on the me-timer who needs space.

All of this feels much more okay when you know who you are and what your basic needs are. It is okay to be how you are. There is not a wrong or right. But if this understanding isn't there, the connector thinks there is something wrong with the me-timer. *Maybe he doesn't really like me? Whatever, he's boring and unfriendly, anyway.* And the me-timer sees the connector as flaky and superficial. Each sees himself as better than the other. We can just realize that everyone has unique needs, instead of being offended or annoyed.

Too Close

There are times when people violate other people's space. We see this when their words and letters are too close. Look at Figure 6-3.

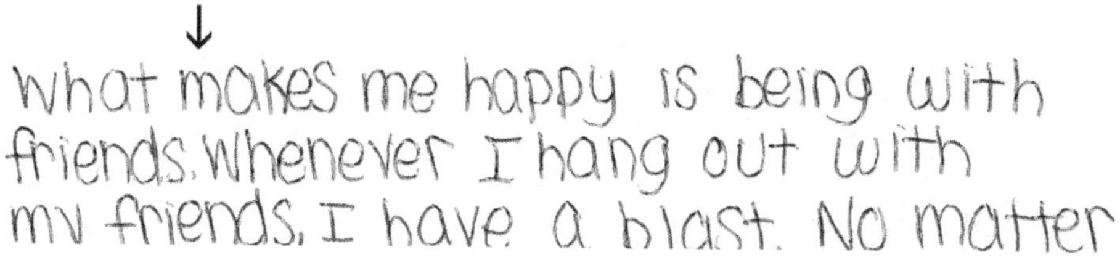

↓
what makes me happy is being with
friends. whenever I hang out with
my friends, I have a blast. No matter

Figure 6-3

They bump into each other. The M in the word "makes" (first line, second word) is twice as large as the space between the words, which are almost touching each other. The F and D in the word "friends" (third line, second word) are almost touching the word above them. We said before that an M-sized space is balanced. A person whose spaces are slightly smaller or larger is still healthy; it just means the person has social needs that go a bit in one direction or the other. But when the words are *too* close, when they invade the space of other letters or words—or even cut them off—then the writer has a deep-seated need to connect, along with a fear that he can't. Feeling desperate to overcome this and thinking only of their own needs, such people forget about the other person's needs. They don't pick up cues that the other guy might feel a little uncomfortable with them. If they are rejected in relationships, they feel like failures, fueling their fears and causing stress and even *more* failure in this area. They're trying to compensate for their perceived social inadequacies, but it's just causing others to want to distance themselves from these people even more. And the cycle continues.

Too Far Apart

Some people have a need for space that is more than that of the average person (Figure 6-4).

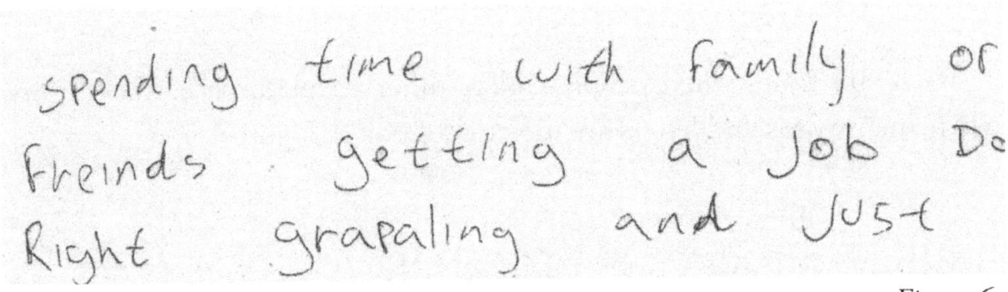

> spending time with family or freinds. getting a job Do Right grapaling and just

Figure 6-4

Look at the extra-large spaces between the words; now see the letter M in the word "time." Two of those M's could fit in the spaces between the words. It could be that he feels uncomfortable with others, maybe that he just really enjoys me-time; either way, the result is the same: This person needs *a lot* of space, more than your regular me-timer. He's not necessarily completely antisocial or socially inept; it could be that he is socially capable and able to be around people and have a good time, as long as it's not too much or too often. Still, as with most extremes, it's important to keep an eye out for this teen, to help him, to love him unconditionally, to support him, and to accept him.

Notes

Chapter Seven

Information Versus Action

A person's handwriting can be divided into three horizontal zones (Figure 7-1). The upper zone represents the intellect; the lower zone represents the emotions,[3] and the middle zone represents how he relates to the present.

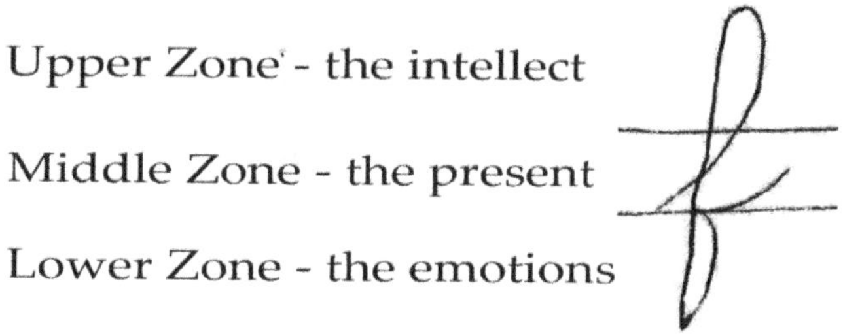

Upper Zone - the intellect

Middle Zone - the present

Lower Zone - the emotions

Figure 7-1

Fun-Lovers

A person with a large middle zone and small to average upper and lower zones is a person who is into action, not details. When a writer's middle zone dominates, you have a person who doesn't like meetings, who doesn't like heavy planning; these people would rather just deal with it all as it comes. They can handle the details if they have to; they're happy to think something through to an extent, but they'd rather not. They are doers.

---

3 *For more on emotions and the lower zone, see* The Complete Idiot's Guide to Handwriting

Unlock: The Secret World of Teenagers

Analysis by Sheila Lowe.

Some writers, more extreme, have very small upper and lower zones (Figure 7-2). These people, the fun-lovers, are self-centered, self-absorbed, in-the-moment people. Where average, action-oriented people can still be thinkers, getting a bit of data and then winging the rest, the fun-lovers are really *not* into thinking; they're not into long-term planning; they're into only acting, behaving. *Don't bother me with the facts; just trying to have a good time over here!*

Many teenagers don't see a tomorrow, they don't see consequences, they don't fear death, and life just is. They don't develop long-term goals yet. Their planning consists of two days from now or *maybe* as far as next week, and fun is the only motivator. *I want to have fun; I don't want to sit and learn details that are not necessary; I want to move; I want to go; I don't care if it's dangerous; it sounds like fun. What about the rest of my life? Who cares! Tomorrow we're going to the beach!*

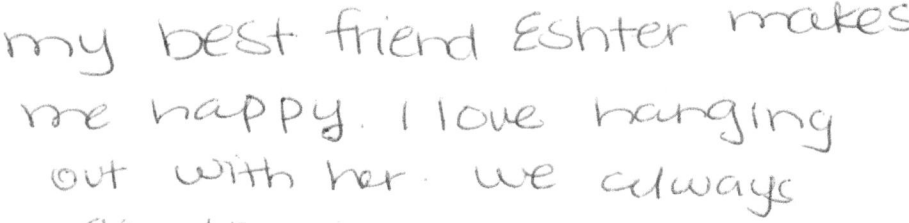

Figure 7-2

Frustrating as this may be for their parents and teachers, this *is* age appropriate for a teenager. The challenge is to help these teenagers to grow older and wiser *within* their innate outlook on life. So they have short attention spans and basically no desire to know details? Okay, work with it. And watch out: Do *not* attempt to compare these fun-loving generalists to their counterparts, the information-seekers (see below). *Why can't you be more like David? He actually likes to do his homework!* These two types have totally different operating systems, and it doesn't help—in fact, it hurts—to compare them.

Information-Seekers

Someone whose writing is very small in all zones (but still in the proper zone ratio) is someone who looks for the details (Figure 7-3). These people want to really understand things; they take their time before acting just to make sure they have all the information they need.

More extreme, some writers have a small middle zone with a large upper zone (Figure 7-4). Even more than the small-writers, the information-seekers are extremely thoughtful; they love and need to acquire knowledge. They want to know all the details and find it extremely difficult to do, often getting stuck in the fear that they don't know enough yet.

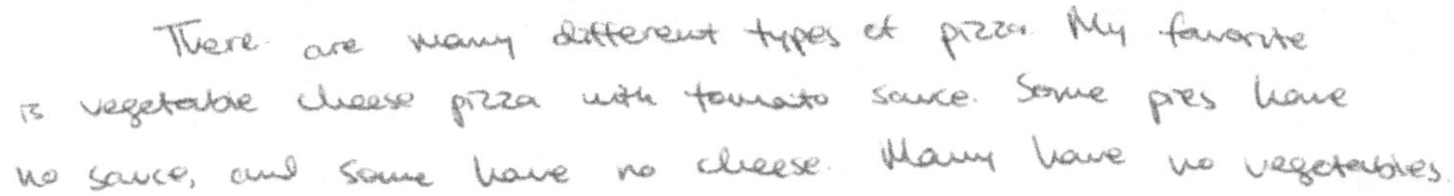

There are many different types of pizza. My favorite is vegetable cheese pizza with tomato sauce. Some pies have no sauce, and some have no cheese. Many have no vegetables.

Figure 7-3

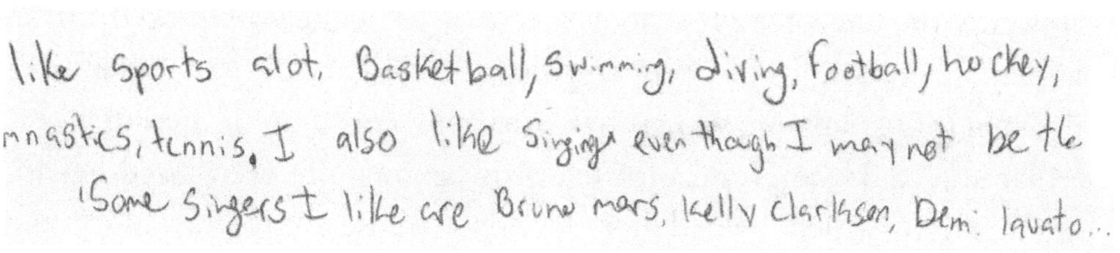

I like sports alot, Basketball, swimming, diving, football, hockey, mnastics, tennis, I also like Singing even though I may not be the Some Singers I like are Bruno mars, Kelly clarkson, Demi lavato...

Figure 7-4

I need to know more, not just for the test, but I want to know what you're talking about; I want to totally understand. What if I'm not prepared? What if I mess up?

Whether a large-writer or a small-writer, a fun-loving generalist or an information-seeker, these tendencies start early on in the teenage years.

Most of it is inborn, meaning there's often little to be done about it except channel the tendencies in the most productive direction. It can be difficult for each group to understand the other. It is not unusual for fun-lovers to think the information-seekers are nerdy, and information-seekers often think the fun- lovers are just a bunch of airheads. These teens need to know that diversity creates growth, and each group can play off of each other's strengths. (Actually, if done right, people with opposing tendencies can work very well with each other: the small-writers do the research, then they give it over to the large- writers to act on it!) The key is for teens from any group to love who they are and appreciate the differences in others.

It can happen that a teen can be supported to the extent that he actually changes his tendencies. Figure 7-5 shows the writing of a 16-year-old girl and the transformation that she made by the time she was 19 years old. At 16, she's a clear fun-lover. Overshadowed by her siblings, she did not get the attention she needed by her parents and sought out external stimulation. She tried to rebel a bit, though she was too much of a rule-follower to get into much trouble. Mainly, she just ignored her responsibilities in preference of having a good time.

Towards the end of high school, a few of her educators picked up on her need for attention and proper guidance. They took her under their wing, mentoring her on a personal level and encouraging her to live a life that she could be proud of. One of these mentors even hired her for a summer job, which helped her develop a sense of responsibility and feel needed, intelligent, and capable. She went to college, found a healthy and supportive group of friends, and started experiencing and enjoying academic success.

Her handwriting samples show that between ages 16 and 19, different aspects of her personality came out. The fun-loving, self-absorbed girl with her large middle-zone letters and close spaces between words was transformed into a young adult whose writing is much more balanced with healthy word

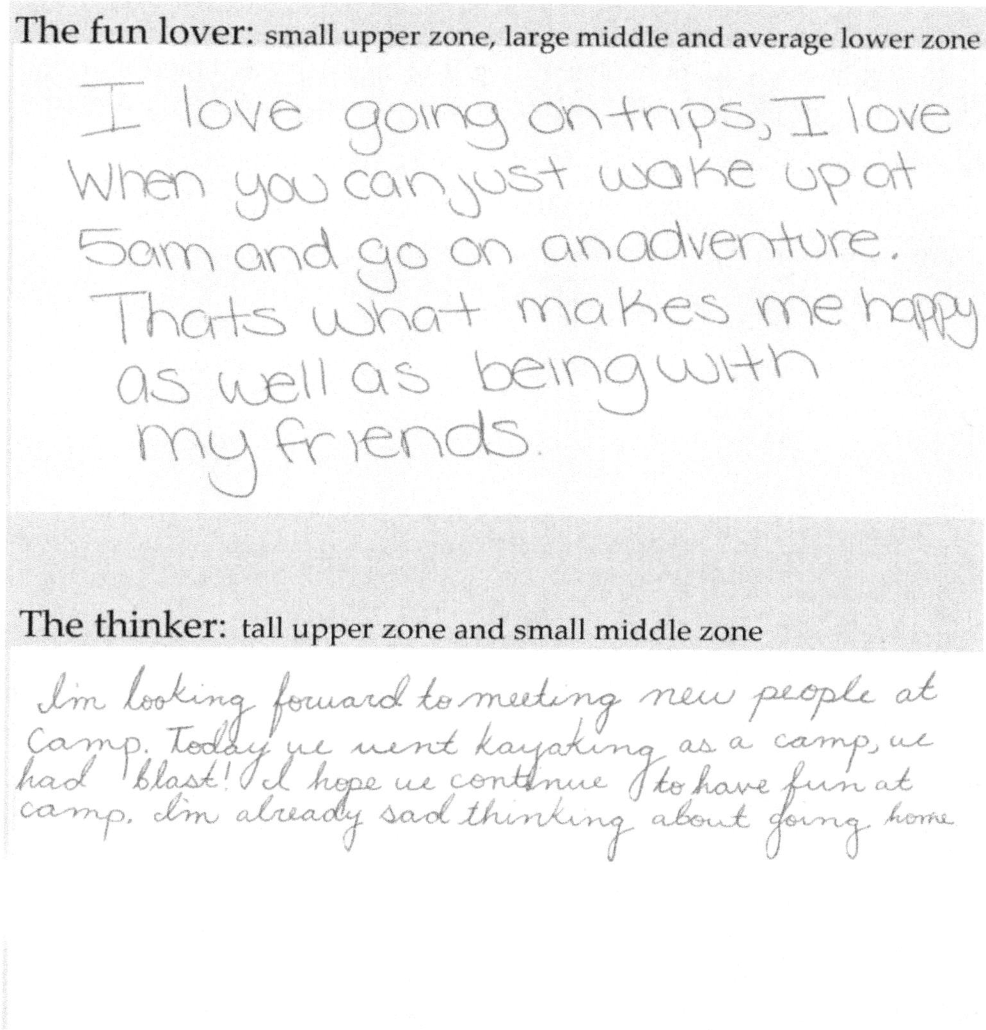

The fun lover: small upper zone, large middle and average lower zone

> I love going on trips, I love when you can just wake up at 5am and go on an adventure. Thats what makes me happy as well as being with my friends.

The thinker: tall upper zone and small middle zone

> I'm looking forward to meeting new people at Camp. Today we went kayaking as a camp, we had a blast! I hope we continue to have fun at camp. I'm already sad thinking about going home

Figure 7-5

spacing and a newly developed upper zone. The new upper zone shows her desire to learn and to use that knowledge to advance her position in life. The smaller middle zone shows that she's become less into herself and more generous with and aware of others. Her 19-year-old self is more confident. Whereas at 16 she had insecure, fearful roller coaster lines of text, now her lines are straight and strong. She is a happier person.

It is important to note that this girl at age 16 was not seeking out change in her life. It was her mentors, the fact that they showed faith in her and encouraged her to become more, that inspired a change of direction and even personality that she herself wasn't looking for. The power of outside support cannot be overstated.

Notes

Chapter Eight

In the I's

Teenagers are just beginning to make a transition from their home as their dominating influence to their friends becoming the dominating influence. The stronger a teenager's bond is with his parents, the more likely he will make prudent choices and not stray far from his family's morals and values. A person's capital I is indicative of his feelings towards his parents and, indirectly, his emotional outlook. There are three basic ways of making the capital letter I (Figure 8-1). The Palmer I Method I is on the left, the Box I in the middle, and the Simple I is on the right. Of course, there are many variations of these three basic forms.

Figure 8-1

Palmer I

When making a Palmer-Method I (Figure 8-2), the writer will start in the lower right corner curving the pen up to the top.[4] Looping back down to the base, the writer then moves the pen out to the left, creating a half circle, before ending the I with the final horizontal movement to the right.

---

4 *Most people form a Palmer-Method "I" in this manner. However, some form it in the opposite direction, i.e., the left portion first and the upright oval portion second. In this case, the information to follow is switched, the upright oval now representing the father, and the leftmost half-circle to the side representing the mother. The same is true for the Box I. Most people form the top bar before the bottom one, but for someone who forms the bottom bar before the top one, the representations of the mother and father switch.*

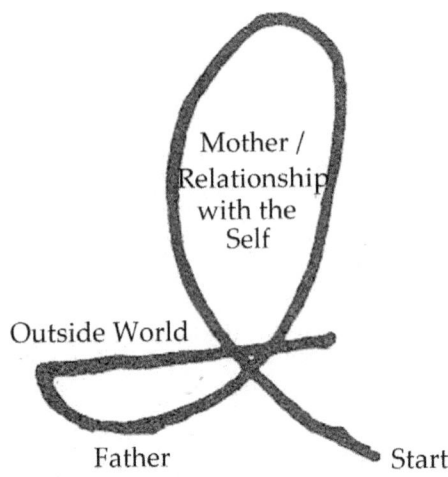

Figure 8-2

The central upright oval represents how the writer feels about his connection to his mother. If this oval is full and open, with an average width being about half the height, the writer feels a healthy, close relationship with his mother. If the oval is very thin, the writer feels his relationship with his mother is lacking. On the other extreme, if this oval is wider than average, the writer is relying too much on the mother, or the mother is too dominant. Any irregular angles or twists in this area represent difficulties in this relationship. Since children learn self-respect and emotional stability primarily from the mother, this portion of the I represents these aspects, as well. Figures 8-3 and 8-4 show a sampling of just a few of the many variations possible for the Palmer I.

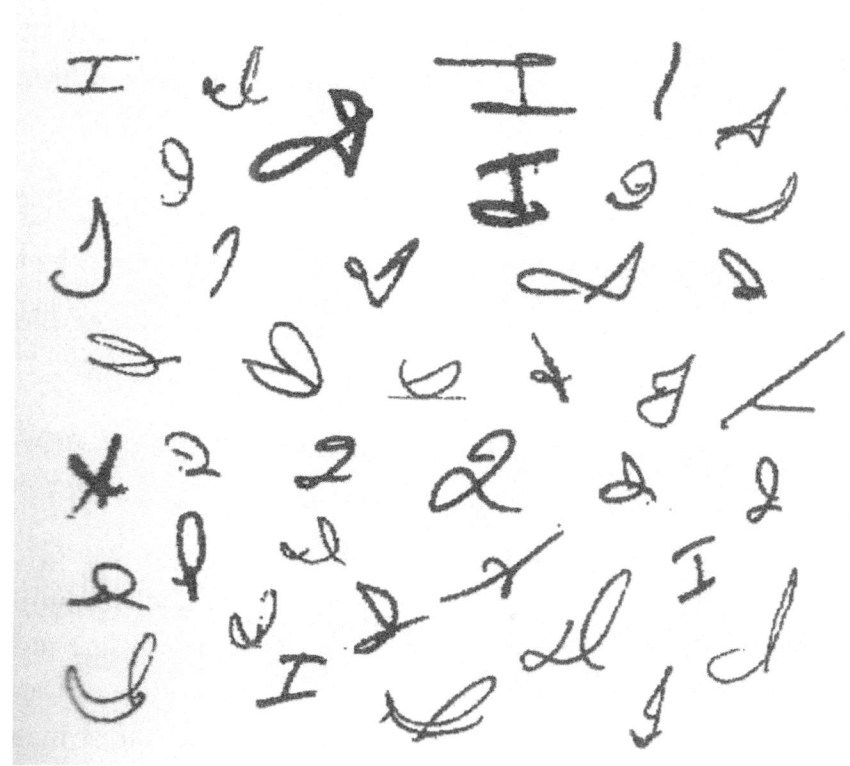

Figure 8-3

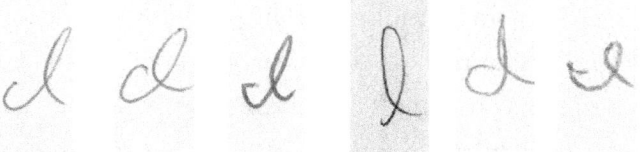

Figure 8-4

The half-circle that juts out to the left represents the writer's relationship with his father. If the round bottom portion of this half-circle is of average size (just smaller than the upper oval representing the mother), the writer's relationship to his father is healthy, and if it is smaller or larger than average, this represents distance from the father or over-reliance on the father, respectively. Also similarly, any extra twists, turns, or angles represent difficulties.

Children learn how to interact with others and the outside world (business knowhow, goal setting, social norms, etc.) primarily from the father.[5] The final horizontal stroke to the right that is formed after the leftmost half-circle, represents the tools the father gave the writer with which to go out into the world. As you could probably guess, the longer and straighter the stroke, the better the tools, unless the line goes much beyond the central intersection of the I, in which case there's some kind of abnormality.

The Box I

The Box I (Figure 8-5) has a vertical line in the middle, a horizontal bar on top, and a horizontal bar on bottom. The vertical line indicates how the person feels about himself. If the vertical line is nice and straight, the person has a healthy self-confidence. Leaning to one side or the other, curves, angles, or any irregular formation of this portion of the I indicates some dissonance with the self. The upper horizontal bar represents the mother and the bottom represents the father. If the upper and lower bars are perfectly even crossing at all the right points, the relationship with the parents is healthy. When one of the horizontal bars doesn't intersect with the vertical bar, this indicates distance between the writer and the parent, or if the bar intersect too far into the vertical line, the writer feels anger, frustration, or misunderstanding directed at the parent. (Figure 8-6)

---

5 *According to Sigmund Freud, when the father leaves the house, the child learns that there is a world outside of the house.*

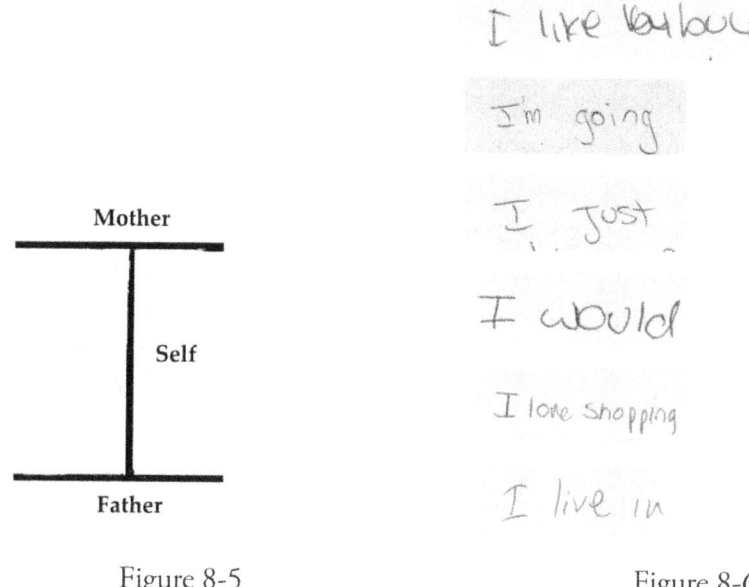

Figure 8-5   Figure 8-6

The Simple I [6]

The Simple I (Figure 8-7) is essentially a Box I with no horizontal bars. As those missing bars represent the writer's mother and father, the Simple I indicates a person for whom the mother and father are, at least in the mind of the writer, simply not present. The writer feels entirely independent, in absolute control of his life. These teenagers handle it all on their own and see no need to inform their parents of anything.

This simple I is the most interesting I when discussing teenagers. Most teenagers have *some* kind of relationship with their parents. It may be close and loving, or it may be argumentative and resentful, but feelings are there in one capacity or another. If someone writes a Palmer I or a Box I, it could be that there are irregularities that represent distance, over-reliance, friction, or some other difficulty, but these Is show *some* sense of involvement, however rocky the relationship may be. Contrastingly, the

---

6   *The information presented about the simple I is not relevant when discussing Australians, who are taught the Simple I as the standard form of this letter.*

teenager who writes a Simple I is essentially saying his parents have no effect on his life whatsoever.

This is not a sign a parent wants to see. The kid who's 13 or 14 who writes a Simple I is usually exhibiting unusually firm independence at all costs. But sometimes this is less personality based and more circumstantial. For example, children who go away to boarding school at a very young age develop this characteristic, though it doesn't necessarily hint to anything unhealthy.

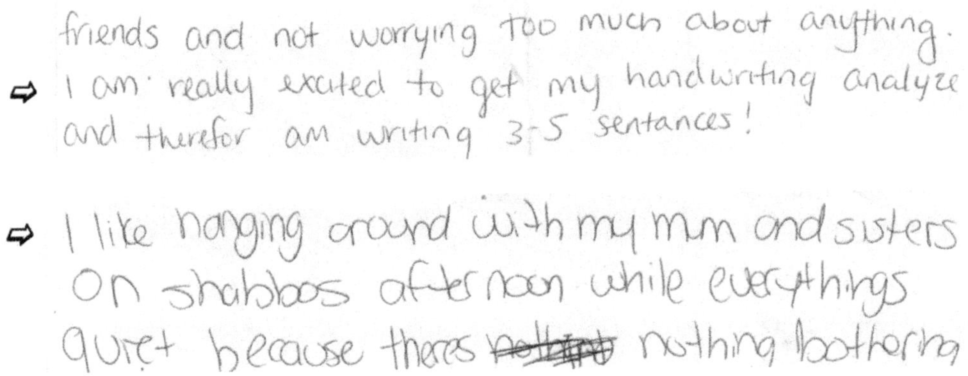

> friends and not worrying too much about anything.
> ➪ I am really excited to get my handwriting analyze and therefor am writing 3-5 sentances!
>
> ➪ I like hanging around with my mm and sisters on shabbos afternoon while everythings quiet because theres ~~nothing~~ nothing bothering

Figure 8-7

Many teens at risk or on the street will write a Simple I. Their independent attitude is often a combined result of strong negative influences at home and an immature yet supportive outside environment. Except in rare cases, this extreme self-reliance is not expected or healthy until the early 20s (and even then, it is not necessarily healthy or normal in every case). Other indicators can be used to tell whether the Simple I is healthy or not. For example, the Simple I in Figure 8-7, which also presents with roller coaster insecurities (see Chapter 3) and blob cross-outs (see Chapter 4), is clearly in need of some guidance.

Figure 8-8 is an example of a teenager who went to boarding school. This teenager has learned to take care of himself. He doesn't have an adult around to help him with his day-to-day needs. His circumstances and inner strength have taught him to become self-sustaining and independent in a way that is beneficial to his life, not detrimental to it.

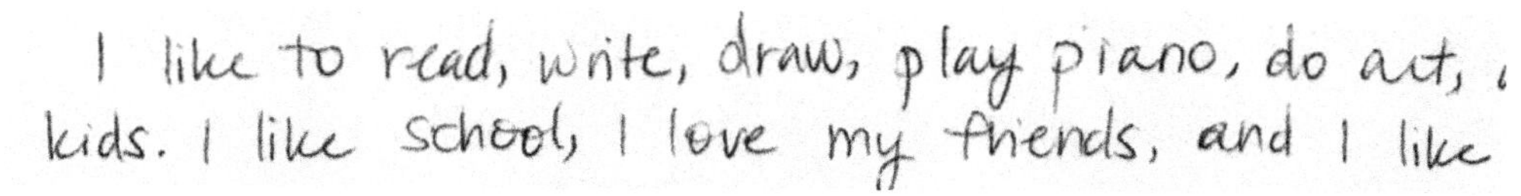

I like to read, write, draw, play piano, do art, kids. I like school, I love my friends, and I like

Figure 8-8

For more information on the letter I, I highly recommend the following titles:

The Complete Idiot's Guide to Handwriting Analysis by Sheila Lowe

You and Your Private I: Personality and the Written Self Image by Jane Nugent Green

Forensic Profiling Cards, created by Kimon Iannetta and James F. Craine, Ph.D.

Notes

Chapter Nine

Combo of Champions:

Competence and Compassion

Mental health is achieved through baby steps. Every tiny success is, in truth, a monumental milestone. And sometimes, these milestones can be met with something as small as a hug, an "I understand," a knowing nod.

We all need lamplighters to brighten our way, to share their light and illuminate the path for us. We thrive when we receive understanding, kindnesses and sensitivities from another. We need people to be there for us, even though we don't always realize it. Our personal lamplighters know when to speak, when to listen, when to be soft, when to be firm, when to give a hug. Lamplighters are not perfect people; they are just genuine, empathetic, and present.

For parents and teachers to become lamplighters, they need two essential tools. The first is compassion; the second, and equally as important, is competence. With compassion alone, it's like being head over heels for your car but not knowing how to drive it. Your love for the car is nice, but it doesn't help you get it to work. The love stays on the surface, and the car doesn't serve its purpose. The love is not enough.

Competence without compassion doesn't work, either. Imagine an air conditioner blowing cold air in the frigid winter months giving steam in the hot summer heat. The air conditioner and furnace both work perfectly, but neither is connected to the present needs.

Teenagers develop trust for their lamplighters when the lamplighters have a combination of compassion *and* competence. With competence, you can see a teenager's roller coaster lines (Chapter 3) and recognize his world, and with compassion, you can explain to the teenager what he's experiencing and how he can work with it. You can comfort the teen by telling him his feelings are age-appropriate and normal. You can inspire him to experience courage, peace, excitement, an open heart, and a clear head, and you can help him understand his need for control and his fear of embarrassment.

The following information will help turn parents and teachers into lamplighters by lending further clarity to certain overarching principles that affect most teens (and most adults, too):

    a. Independence is in the eye of the beholder
    b. Our strengths are our weaknesses
    c. Good surrounds us; negativity pierces us
    d. The bell curve

Notes

Chapter Ten

Guiding Principles

Independence Is in the Eye of the Beholder

Remember the roller coaster writers from Chapter Four? By now, you know that this points to the writer's waxing and waning confidence in his ability to do what he wants or needs to do (Figure 10-1). This unresolved and constantly changing state causes teens to act erratically. They can feel great one moment and awful the next. It is personal, deep, and exhausting to them. They are on a roller coaster.

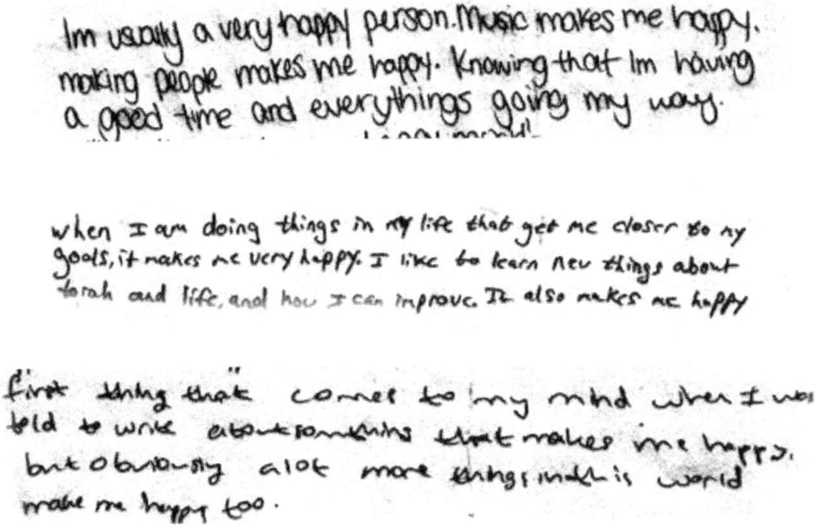

> Im usually a very happy person. Music makes me happy. making people makes me happy. Knowing that Im having a good time and everythings going my way.

> when I am doing things in my life that get me closer to my goals, it makes me very happy. I like to learn new things about torah and life, and how I can improve. It also makes me happy

> first thing that comes to my mind when I was told to write about something that makes me happy, but obviously alot more things in this world make me happy too.

Figure 10-1

When a child hits his teenage years, he is seeing himself as a singular entity for the first time. This comes with more privileges and more responsibilities, and this change often gives teens the impression that they are now entitled to ultimate independence, that they're smart enough and wise enough to be free of the reign of their parents, teachers, and all other forms of authority. Problem is, they're wrong. They are *not* developed enough to be able to run their own lives exactly as they see fit. For that matter, neither are adults. This is why we have laws. You can explain this. *Honey, even Mommy isn't independent. I have to stop at the red lights and go at the green lights. Am I always in the mood to stop when I see a red light? Of course not! But if I don't, someone could get hurt.* All people need rules to varying degrees, each person according to his own level, increasing with proven responsibility, but the *total* independence that they are fighting so desperately for is something that does not truly exist.

Teens need to be made aware that parents and teachers enforce rules not because of a power trip but because it is for the teen's benefit, even if it doesn't always feel like it. At the same time, the teens need to be given some sense of autonomy, too. The more unnecessary control an adult tries to impose upon a teen, the more the teen will push back, frustrating the adult and making him want to control the teen even more. Of course it's aggravating and even painful when parents try to help and guide their children, and the children, like a slap in the face, want none of it, negating all the parents have done for them to bring them to this point in their maturity. But feeding the power struggle creates a great divide, impeding trust on both ends and ultimately defeating the true goal of *both* parties: helping the teenager to learn to live like an adult.

Is it scary? You bet! How many parents have gazed at their three-year-old and wondered whether the child would ever cross the street by himself? *I can't see it,* they think. Now obviously when that three-year-old turns 14, it isn't even a thought. Somewhere along the way, he became capable of crossing the street alone. And somewhere along the way, he will become capable of doing *all* the things he needs to do, if you let him learn.

Communicate to your teen that he will be given more autonomy as he demonstrates responsible behavior. You will feel safe knowing that the limits you place on your teen are stage-appropriate, and your teen will know what is expected of him to get what he wants. During the late teen years or early twenties, most people begin to understand their parents' motives. They become less volatile and more secure with themselves. Those arbitrary rules are not so arbitrary; they see that the guidance their parents imposed upon them were only there to help the teens develop into happy, healthy adults. It is no longer the teenager against his parents; rather, the teenager is now an active participant in his own growth.

Teenagers are trying to act knowledgeable and experienced even though they usually lack both traits. Many times they are negotiating some specific event, moral issue or life style preference for the first time, without a full picture of the consequences of their choices. This is normal and they are going to make mistakes, sometimes big mistakes. These mistakes can be like falling into a pit. The pit can become their new identity. Now they are prepared to defend their new position. It is theirs. Embarrassment, scared anxiety, rejection, fear, worthlessness, false pride, insecurity, humiliation, betrayal or any other emotion causes them to invest in the limits of the pit environment instead of crawling out. Crawling out would allow them to learn the lessons of their actions and move on a bit wiser. We need to encourage them that they are normal and that their desires to be in charge of their destiny are normal. We need to let them know that mistakes don't define them, rather, it's how they handle the mistake that does. Our conversation with them goes like this; "We are glad you want to be in charge of your own destiny. From our experience, may we make a suggestion of what we think your next move should be?" (Pause and wait for the response.) We need to show compassion as well as demonstrate competence in order to create trust between ourselves and our teens in order to help them learn, grow, and respect themselves.

Our Strengths Are Our Weaknesses

Whether a talented painter, a kind friend, an excellent student, or what have you, people hold onto their strengths as the backbone of who they are. But at some point, all people are tested with the challenge of determining whether the trait by which they identify themselves is appropriate to exhibit in every single circumstance. As an example, let's take the smartest kid in the class who sees his greatest strength as his intelligence. What happens when Mr. Intelligent doesn't know something? He might have a hard time asking for help, because it goes against his definition of who he is. I'm the smartest kid in the class; how can I not figure this out on my own? Meanwhile, instead of using his intelligence as a crutch, something that is not to his benefit and does not make him smarter, he can learn so much more if he'd just ask for help when he needs it.

What about the nicest girl in the class who never says no to anyone? What if a questionable character were to approach her outside of school, asking her to come with him? She would be scared, feeling that something might be wrong here, but she would feel bad because she doesn't want to be mean. Clearly, it's the wrong choice to put her safety in the hands of a shady stranger just because she feels like she has to be nice!

Help your teenagers understand that if they define themselves too heavily by their strengths and rely on these strengths at a time that's inappropriate, these strengths can become major weaknesses. But, by the same token, when they identify a moment where they can tap into what they perceive to be a weakness when the moment calls for it, that perceived weaknesses can become a new strength. Show them that to everything, there is a season. There are times to be strong, and there are times to be vulnerable. There are times to rely on one's own knowledge, and there are times to call on the wisdom of others. There are time to be distant, and there are times to connect. When someone learns to seize the right moment to use his "weaknesses," he becomes a more whole person who is able to be fluid in many circumstances. Learning to act in accordance with the needs of the moment at hand is what makes a capable, thriving adult.

Good Surrounds Us and Negativity Pierces Us

Picture this: You're at an internationally acclaimed steakhouse that boasts the best flavors you could ever hope to savor. You're anticipating the most succulent five-course meal of your life. True to your expectations, the appetizer is out of this world. Following it is a tantalizing, delightfully unusual salad, and then a hearty soup that would put even your grandmother to shame. The steak from the main course is even more divine than you could have imagined, cooked to dreamlike perfection. The steak-fries that came with the main course are a little oily, but it's not like you are still hungry, anyway. But of course, there's always room for dessert, which is so decadent that a cherry on top would be an insult.

Upon leaving the restaurant, having eaten what was easily the best meal you've ever had in your life, you run into a friend who's about to go into the same restaurant. "How was it?" he asks. "It was amazing," you answer, "but watch out for the fries, they were way too oily. I mean seriously, at the world's best restaurant, how can you mess up fries?"

Now tell me, what's wrong with this picture? The fries were a hundred percent irrelevant to the meal. If they hadn't been served, they wouldn't have been missed. And they were extra to begin with; you didn't even order them! But in your mind, you're not giving a complete account of what happened if you don't mention the mediocre fries. In fact, the fries are the *only* item that you mention specifically, even though the satisfaction you experienced from the delicious parts of the meal was certainly greater than the dissatisfaction you experienced from the fries. And yet, the fact remains: the fries have more strength than all the other dishes that you enjoyed.

The good things that happen to us have a tendency to affect us only externally. Instead of penetrating us, they surround us, making us feel comfortable for a while, but not for long. Their effects are often only skin- deep. As the expression goes, "I feel good all over." The goodness surrounds you, but it doesn't get in.

Contrastingly, when something bad happens, it drives straight through to your insides, and if you don't do something very deliberate to yank it out, you can bet it's gonna stay there. "You pierced my heart," as they say. Negative events affect our outlook on life in a more profound way than positive ones do.

The goal is to switch it, to get the positivity to penetrate, and to let the negativity hover above and dissipate. While any person is prone to letting negativity reign, teens especially can totally disregard the good things happening to them when even one little thing goes wrong. Remind them, without belittling their feelings, that the good that happens to them is far more significant (and likely even more frequent) than the few undesirable things.

While this is true for the things that happen *to* the teen, the same is of course true for who the teen *is*. We naturally let our strengths get clouded over by our failures. A baseball player might have hit three home runs, but if he strikes out once, he bums out. If a kid gets a 99 on the test, he beats himself up for missing that one question. (See Chapter 11 for more on the self-defeating personality type that I call OWE, Own Worst Enemy.) Look out for big blob writers who feel they need to cover up if they make a faux-pas, and watch also for the large-margin people, who are scared of approaching the future or past. Also keep an eye open for small-writers who fear missing a detail and failing because of it.

Repeat to your teens that there's nothing wrong with mistakes, especially if the effort is there to learn from them for next time around.

You're not a 50 just because you scored a 50 on the test; the test is just a guide so you know what to work on for next time. Mistakes are great; they give us direction for life's most valuable lessons.

And while telling them that the bad's not so bad, don't forget to tell them that the good is great. They need to be told that their positive qualities matter, a lot. They need to appreciate and internalize what they do well, even the tiny things. If the kid's average goes from a 65 to a 70, congratulate him. If his handwriting is very clear, praise him for it. If he goes an hour without bothering his brother, thank him for it. Teach your teens to pierce their hearts with their goodness, joy, and confidence.

"While one person hesitates because he feels inferior, the other is busy making mistakes and becoming superior."

__Henry C. Link__

"Freedom is not worth having if it does not include the freedom to make mistakes."

__Mahatma Gandhi__

"The greatest mistake you can make in life is to be continually fearing you will make one."

__Elbert Hubbard__

"The best part about making mistakes is that the insane things that we did, those hysterical mistakes, those stupid things that we did when we were young, are our best stories when we get older."

__Unknown__

The Bell Curve Rule

Populations show similar patterns. See the bell curve in Figure 10-2 (numbers rounded): there is the average, representing the majority, and there are the positive and negative extremes.

Bell Curve 90/10 Rule

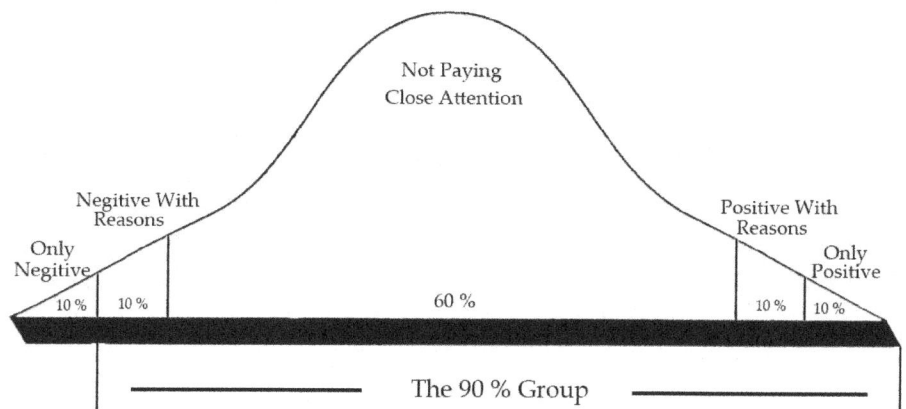

Figure 10-2

During any event, happening, speech, picnic, etc., the people participating will fall into five general groups. The first group (10 percent of all participants) is made up of people who are unconditionally positive. No matter what is happening, they just love it. The second group (also 10 percent) feels conditionally positive; they have reasons why they like what's going on. Those in the third and largest group (60 percent) are neutral or apathetic. These people are too busy with other aspects of their lives to spend much time having an opinion here. Those in the fourth group (10 percent) don't like what's going on and have their reasons, and the fifth group (10 percent) doesn't like the situation for no reason at all.

Let's say a hundred people go to a lecture. Roughly, 10 people will love the talk before they even get there. Ten will like the lecture and will have really thought into why. Sixty will be uncommitted; the lecture was okay, alright, whatever. Ten will not like the lecture; they will have some specific criticism, some of it helpful. The last 10 will hate the talk without cause.

Here's where the bell curve rule comes in. The first four groups, 90 percent, are made up of people who are either supportive and positive, have some kind of constructive feedback to offer, or don't have anything to say either way. Ten percent will always be negative just to be negative. So why worry about them.

I was once riding a bicycle and stopped at a retaining wall. Hardly dressed for the occasion and overweight by a good 40 pounds, I was in a business suit with a helmet and glasses. I pushed off from the retaining wall, reaching with my right foot for the pedal... but I missed it. My foot slipped, throwing me off balance, and I toppled to the ground.

In front of me were about a hundred people doing their own thing, spending their day in the sun. And there I was, lying on the ground for everyone to see. I wondered, *what are these people going to think of me?*

Having read about the bell curve, I knew that in this crowd were 10 people who would never like me no matter what I did. To those ten, I was nothing but a fat, clumsy, funny looking, poorly dressed klutz, a waste of a human being. It was no use trying to impress these people, so I forgot about them. I also knew that there were 10 other people in the crowd on the opposite end of the spectrum who just loved humanity and cared for everyone. The moment I fell, their instant love of G-d's creatures surely came out. Those people would be overcome with worry as to whether I was okay, whether I'd broken anything, and how they must help somehow. There would be 10 more who felt for me because they'd thought about the circumstances (*Poor guy, wearing a suit and everything!*), ten who thought I was a fool because they'd also thought about the circumstances (*Well, he kind of had it coming to him... Who wears a suit on a bike?*), and 60 who had their own lives, to whom my existence wouldn't really make a difference. They'd see me fall. They'd mentally make a note, *I did that once,* and then they'd go back to what they were doing without giving me a second thought.

With 20 percent who thought I was a loser, 60 percent who didn't think anything about me at all, and 20 percent who loved me, that's 80 percent of people who felt neutral to positive about me. Pretty good! So I got up, checked to see whether I was okay, and then went about the rest of my day.

When we deal with the margin writers who are afraid of not being liked and of what others will think, or the blob people who are scared of others seeing their mistakes, or the Simple-I writers who have impressions to keep up since they're all on their own, the bell curve comes and says not to worry. We think everyone's thinking bad things about us, but, in reality, it's just not true. We feel we have to go out of our way to impress everyone, but with 80 percent who at worst don't care and at best love us as we are, there's no point in trying to impress anyone. Being ourselves, complete with all our flaws, is the best thing we can do.

How many times has a jerk taken away somebody's dreams? His voice should not matter at all. So many make the mistake of fruitlessly worrying about what the negative 10-percenters will think. Teenagers, extra-sensitive to the negative, need to understand that not every voice is important. Loved ones are honest, present, caring, and helpful. These are the voices who matter.

Notes

Chapter Eleven

Putting It All Together

To analyze a person's handwriting,[7] you have to first know what individual indicators to look for, and then you have to look at all of the indicators as parts of one whole. Part of a (good) graphologist's job is to understand how those indicators mesh with each other, and how to communicate the ideas in a way that is helpful. The more indicators that are found, the more detailed and precise the analysis can be. It's important to practice recognizing the indicators. Once recognizing the indicators becomes more natural, putting them together becomes simpler, as well.

Let's try to do one together here (Figure 11-1). This sample is from a 15-year-old boy. What indicators do you see?

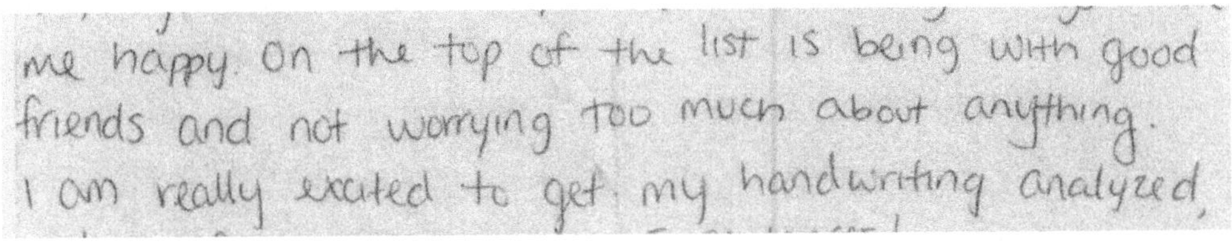

Figure 11-1

Now let's look at each individual indicator on its own.

The roller coaster writing tells us that the teenager is unsure of his status in life; he doesn't feel secure within himself.

Notice the roller coaster, the words that are far apart, and the edge-to- edge writing.

---

7 *To learn more about graphology, I recommend* The Complete Idiot's Guide to Handwriting Analysis *by Sheila Lowe.*

The large spaces between words tell us that he needs a good amount of private time.

The edge-to-edge writing tells us that he doesn't want to listen to authority.

Now let's put all the indicators—and what they indicate—together. The teenager is a self-proclaimed, self-reliant and worried individual. He is afraid to show vulnerability and is desperately trying to keep control. Relying on peers for insight and guidance, he isolates himself from adults, the only real outlet capable of helping him, unless an adult is able to break through his guard and develop trust with him.

So how *do* you help him?

First, tell him that he, and his situation, are completely normal. It is normal for a teenager not to understand his future or have a firm direction. This is not a personality flaw; it's an expected growth path. Next, acknowledge his need for alone time. Explain to him that different people replenish their energy in different ways, and his need for space is a natural, normal, and necessary thing for him; it's the gift he gives himself. At the same time, acknowledge that while he might need time on his own, it's still true that teenagers, or, for that matter, people of any age, often require new, outside perspectives in order to learn and grow, and that getting this from someone who has some life experience and wisdom is probably the way to go. So, this teen might be wary of adults and prefer to vent to his friends, but usually, teen peers cannot offer anything new; they have only like experiences to share, with little real wisdom or understanding surrounding any of it. With sensitivity, ask him if he knows an adult who he's comfortable talking to. And, by the way, even if that person isn't you, your mere acknowledgment that you understand what he's going through is going to make him more relaxed around you and *will* lead to more trust, towards you and maybe even adults in general.

In short, the message he needs to hear is: *Life's ups and downs can be confusing, and I get that you might need some time alone to recharge and deal with it all. That's totally fine. But another equally necessary part of dealing with the roller coaster is learning from those who've been there, stepping outside of your personal box and getting a fresh perspective. Friends can be great support, but a trustworthy adult with some experience under his belt can offer great guidance.*

Now let's try a sample of a 15-year-old girl (Figure 11-2). What do you notice here?

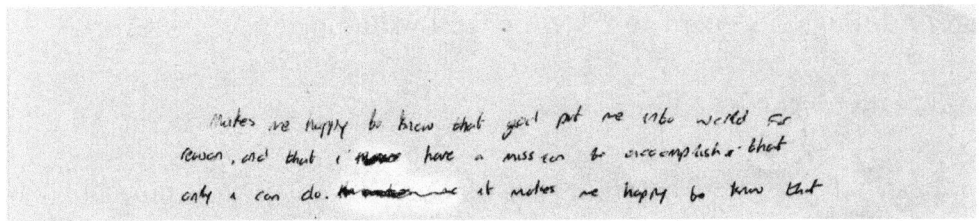

Figure 11-2

Notice the small middle-zone writing, the blobs, and the large margins, plus the distance between words, somewhat illegible writing, and roller coaster.

The small middle-zone writing reflects the writer's intellect and desire to internalize detailed information.

The blobs indicate that she's very worried about making mistakes and about what other people think of her.

The large margins show that she's cautious in new environments and with new ideas.

The distance between the words and the semi-illegible writing indicate her need for private space, and also that she has difficulty communicating with others.

The roller coaster writing shows she doubts her self-worth.

Putting it together, we see a very smart but self-conscious, socially un- comfortable girl who gathers as much information as possible to compensate for her self-doubt, fear of integrating new things into her life, and making mistakes.

To help this girl, compliment her on her intellect, but tell her it's okay to be wrong sometimes, too. Show her you're not judging her by explaining that her mistakes don't define her, that mistakes breed growth, and that what counts is how she handles these mistakes when they inevitably do happen, as they do to everyone. Remind her of the 90/10 rule, reinforcing the idea that the only outside opinions that matter are the ones from her inner circle. She doesn't need to feel the pressure of catering to the entire world. Help her increase her self-awareness by talking to her about negativity's ability to pierce while the good stays only at surface level, even when this is unreasonable and causes people to blow unpleasant things out of proportion. Tell her that instead of hiding behind her intellect as a self-protection device, she can use it to add to her self-awareness and personal growth.

In short: *You're smart; I don't have to tell you that everyone makes mistakes, and all you have to do is use them to grow instead of being afraid of them. Yes, some people might not make you feel great when you mess up, but those people don't matter; they're going to think what they think no matter what you do, so forget about them. Focus on the positive instead of living in the negative and you will flourish.*

Notes

Chapter Twelve

OWE to BFF

One very common personality I see when meeting with teens is something I call OWE — Own Worst Enemy.

An OWE is someone who has a distortedly low self-worth. He is talented and capable, but self-loathing. No matter how outstanding he is, he sees himself so lowly that he has no perception of his own true value. He feels beyond hope or help, and this weighs heavily on him.

Every positive statement about himself is followed by a "but", *I'm an okay athlete, but I'm not as good as Aaron. I'm the best in my class, but that's only because the other kids aren't that smart.* For an OWE, the "but" is bigger than the positive reality. No matter how insignificant it is to an outsider, for an OWE, any slight imperfection completely undermines all of his good traits.

Let's say an OWE had a role in his school play. He would only remember the one line he said wrong, instead of all the ones he recited perfectly. Even if nobody else even noticed it, when complimented on what a great job he did, he'd respond, "Thanks, but I know I messed up on that one line." He feels obligated to announce and emphasize the negative in the name of being "honest," as he believes that his true self is his lowest attribute. Even if he is able to acknowledge that something he did was good, he believes it's not the real him, that the negative is the reality, while the positive is just incidental, a fluke.

An OWE worries incessantly about what others think of him (or what he *thinks* others are thinking of him), as he believes he is only valuable if others see him as such. He constantly looks for outside confirmation of his true worth, but, assuming everyone thinks the worst of him, he falsifies the extent to which other people even notice his faults. For example, imagine an OWE girl who has just been told by her crush that he doesn't want to go out with her. Instead of going on with life as usual, she would hide at home for fear that everyone around her would be staring at her, judging her, thinking she's a loser whom nobody likes. Of course, any person who is rejected might feel insecure at first, but an OWE would continue on like this at length instead of moving on once she realizes this fear is unreasonable and irrelevant.

Because an OWE sees his only value as being that which others find in him, he craves compliments. But because of his poor self-image, he doesn't believe a compliment when he receives it, and instead, he's only reminded of what he's lacking. "You look pretty" elicits the response, "Yeah, but I don't feel pretty." The OWE assumes one of two things: either the person giving the compliment has poor taste and doesn't know what real quality is, or he was only giving the compliment patronizingly, to humor the OWE. Accepting the compliment would show an emotional *need* for a pat on the back, and need implies weakness.

An OWE sees any lack of knowledge as a flaw. This keeps him from asking questions because being taught something means he was lacking something to begin with (notice the edge-to-edge writing and Simple I in Figure 12-1; see Chapters 3 and 8 for more information). Take, for example, an OWE in his first day of chemistry class, afraid to ask the teacher something about the lesson. Even though he has never learned chemistry in his life, and it is even *expected* that he not know anything about the subject, he is afraid to ask, because it will show that there is something he doesn't know.

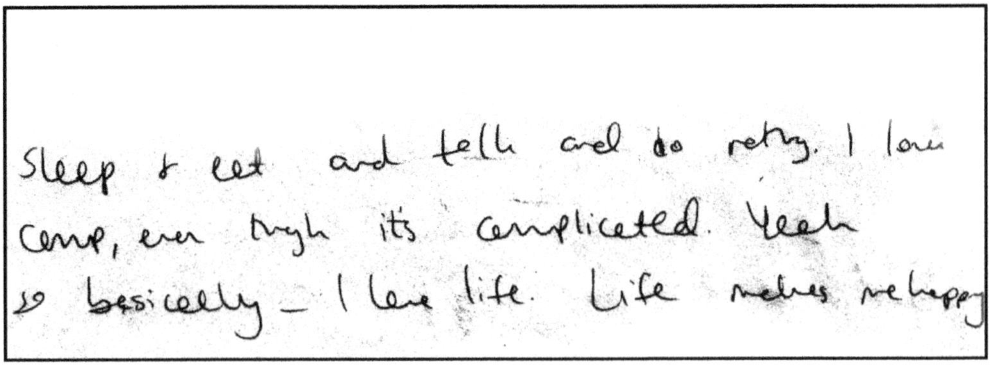

> Sleep & eat and talk and do retry. I love
> comp, even tngh its complicated. Yeah
> so basically — I love life. Life makes me happy

Figure 12-1

An OWE sees himself as being responsible for absolutely everything. This terrifies him because it makes him vulnerable; anything that could go wrong is his fault. An OWE is not only afraid he might fail; he's certain that he *will* fail, so he's hesitant to succeed in anything for fear that he won't be able to duplicate the success. When he does succeed, he deflects it. All positive events are attributed to others, and all negative events are attributed to himself. Anything that goes wrong is, in the eyes of an OWE, his fault; he did something bad, or he should have been able to prevent the bad thing from happening.

Do You Know an OWE?

Lack of knowledge, a need for emotional support, social faux-pas, or any other uncomfortable situation can cause an OWE to turn on certain specific defenses to self-protect and cover up perceived flaws. The OWE either runs away from situations that make him feel vulnerable, or he feigns confidence when he feels weak. Though these defenses can vary, they are often similar and recurring. You can usually identify an OWE if he exhibits any of the following characteristics:

Talented

Perfectionist

Pessimistic

"Tough guy" persona

"I don't care" attitude

Know-it-all

Underachiever

Self-critical

Has difficulty accepting compliments

Overly happy or arrogant

Reluctant to try things or participate

Avoids challenges

Easily overwhelmed

Feels misunderstood

Fears failure

Feels hopeless

Feels unimportant and useless

Feels damaged

Usual Causes of OWE

The cause is usually environmental. Most likely, early in the OWE's life, someone made him feel that he was not good enough. The event could have been real, or imagined. It could have occurred with someone close to him, or someone distant. It could have been a one-time comment, or it could have been something that was repeated many times. It is a common personality type of younger siblings who constantly hear praise of their older brothers and sisters. Even if the younger child is *also* receiving praise, and even if the parents never insinuate that the child is not as good as his older siblings, the younger child often feels he will never be as good as his accomplished brothers and sisters, and thus, an OWE is "born."

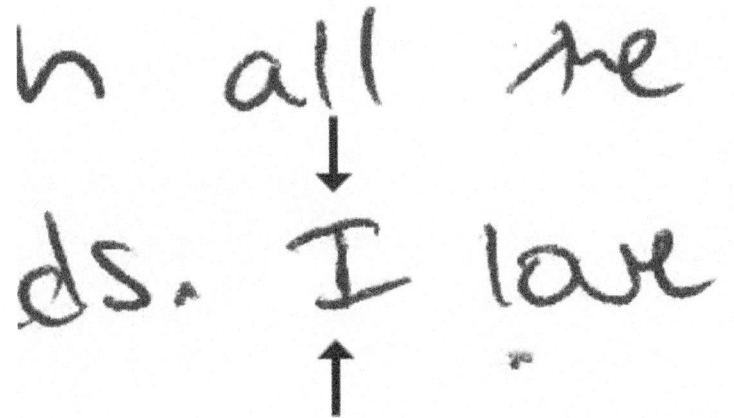

Figure 12-2

Figure 12-3

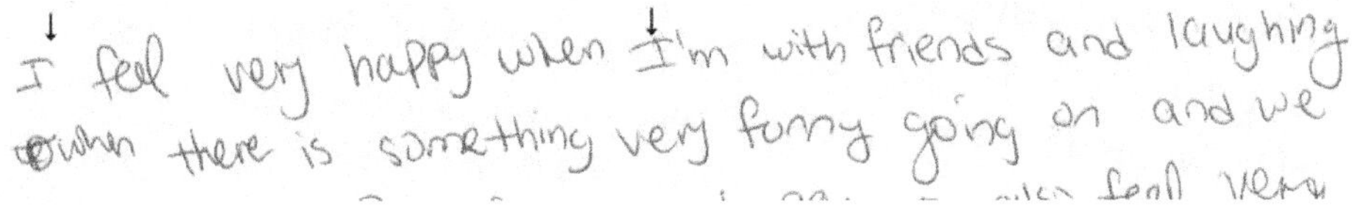

Figure 12-4

Indications of OWE tendencies in Handwriting:[8]

Letter I looks like a 2 (Figure 12-2)

Letter I has concave top or bottom (Figures 12-3, 12-4)

---

8 *Must have two or three signs to make a proper "diagnosis," as not all signs are exclusive to OWE on their own and depend on other factors.*

- Signature is on left side of page
- Signature is very different from handwriting
- Wide right margin
- Wide left and right margins
- Left margin is higher than right
- Small upper margin with no left or right margin
- Blobs
- Line ends on the right higher than where it started on the left

What is the cure?

An OWE just needs to be reprogrammed to think differently about himself. As parents and teachers, we must flood an OWE with positivity. Instead of rebuking or punishing him for making mistakes, we have to assure him that mistakes are normal, that *he* is normal. We must lovingly encourage him and assure him that he is capable of succeeding. In some situations, a teacher might realize that an OWE does not have parents who are capable of giving him the attention he needs. In this case, it is a good idea to find an "adopted" aunt or uncle, an adult figure who can give him caring support and attention on a regular basis. In some situations, it might be necessary to engage in formal therapy or coaching. The road to a successful reprogramming might be longer for some than others, but with time and repetitive diligence from the OWE himself and those around him, no OWE is doomed to be an OWE for life.

Notes

Chapter Thirteen

Abuse: The Life Changer

If a child feels violated, it can change everything about him. You can have a perfectly sweet, motivated, helpful child, and, all of a sudden, one day he becomes mean, uncooperative, defensive, and aloof. This is often the result of some kind of abusive trauma. The child's true sweet self is still there, but it is buried deep underneath the painful memories of the violation. Keep in mind that the violation we're discussing is *perceived*; it's all about how the child *feels* about the incident, not about its objective severity, and so it's difficult to recognize in handwriting the extent of the violation. The trauma presenting in the handwriting could be as benign as somebody stealing a banana from a kindergartener, or as real as sexual abuse. But regardless of whether the perceived abuse was verbal, physical, sexual, financial, or otherwise, these past abusive events create strong emotions that can totally control the present.

Every memory of abuse has an emotion attached to it. Over time, the emotions associated with those memories can radiate with even more pain than there was at the time of the event itself. They become toxic, affecting the teenager to his core, whether he realizes it or not. The emotions can hide in the subconscious, or they can be out in the open to the point that they are totally affecting the teen's behavior in an obvious way. The saying goes that time heals all, but in the case of abuse, time only exacerbates the issue if the person is not working on it head on.

I met Jill when she was 23. I saw in her handwriting that some kind of abuse had taken place when she was a teenager, but she had no recollection of any such event. During the next seven years, she went through a very difficult time getting married and subsequently divorced, and eventually she sought therapy. It was then that she realized that she had, in fact, been abused when she was 13. The abuse hadn't been her fault, but it had affected her until her adult years and into her marriage, without her ever realizing it until the marriage had ended.

Indicators

It should be noted that the scope of this book is not wide enough to cover the complex subject of abuse in its entirety. This chapter is meant only to give some basic information in order to identify when there might be a problem. For our purposes, I have isolated a few basic abuse indicators (Figure 13-1):

Retracing (see the O in "love"): trust issues

Double loops (see the O's in "look"): putting up a guard to self-protect

Lines of text connecting vertically (see "my" in Line 3 touching "listen"

in
Line 4): frustration, antsy dissatisfaction, desires not being met

Bottom end-stroke of Y curves abruptly to the right, or Y has narrow loop, fat, low loop, or angled loop: trauma

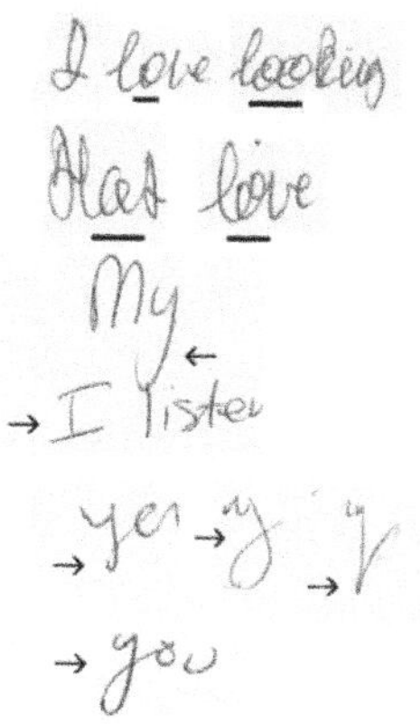

Figure 13-1

Look at the letter Y in Figure 13-2. When the U part is complete, the writer draws the final longer stroke that's drawn downward and then turns clockwise back upward. A healthy Y turns back on itself and points to the right, crossing back over the downward straight line in alignment with the bottom of the U portion of the Y (see Line 6 of Figure 13-1). But if this final rightward stroke stops short of the bottom of the U and makes an abrupt, hard right turn, crossing over the downward line too far below the bottom of the U, this indicates some form of perceived abuse.

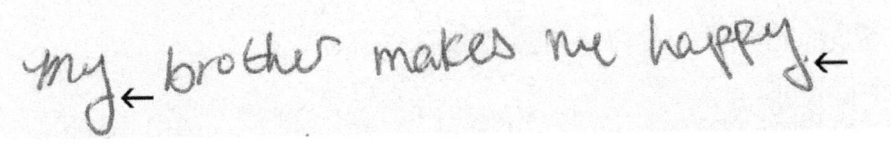

Figure 13-2

We can use the downward rightmost stroke of the Y as a timeline, with the part aligned with the bottom of the U representing the writer at present day, and the bottom of the Y representing the writer at age zero. If the bottom of the writer's Y curves up to the right, look at where that curvature ends in relation to the Y timeline. See the last Y in Line 5; let's say the writer is 15 years old. Since the Y crosses itself about a fifth of the way up from the bottom, we can assume that he endured some kind of trauma around age three.

See Figure 13-2. The writer is a 16-year-old girl whose parents went through a nasty divorce when she was eight years old. Notice the Y in "my" and "happy." the timeline is crossed right in the middle, around age eight. As she gets older, perhaps she will work on herself, go through some kind of therapy, etc., and release the negative emotions associated with the event. If so, then her Y will no longer exhibit signs of trauma. However, if she does not process the negative effects the divorce had on her and keeps them locked up inside, the cross will remain and will occur lower down on her timeline as she ages. By age 24, it will cross around the one-third mark. By age 45, the cross will be very low on the timeline.

Cases

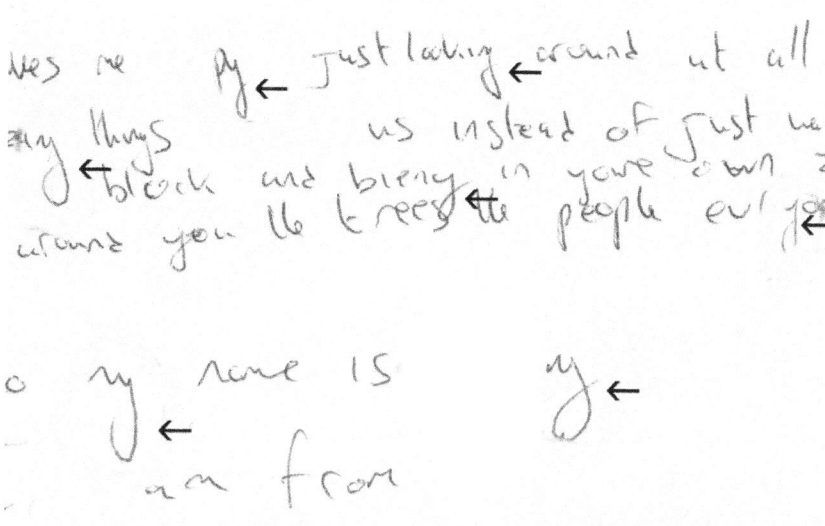

Figure 13-3

Take the example of 18-year-old Darin (Figure 13-3). His father is a respected college professor, student advisor, and community leader. To the public, Darin's father appears to kind, pleasant, and compassionate. But when Darin's father would arrive home in the evening, he was quite different from his public persona. He had a very short fuse, and Darin was his target. He abused Darin verbally, and sometimes physically from the time Darin was four until he was sixteen.

The black arrows pointing to Darin's Ys indicate emotional shutdown at around age four. At 18, Darin started to make improvements. He began talking about the abuse, which enabled him to gain clarity on the issue. After significant therapy, by age 22, Darin's handwriting shows drastic headway (Figure 13-4).

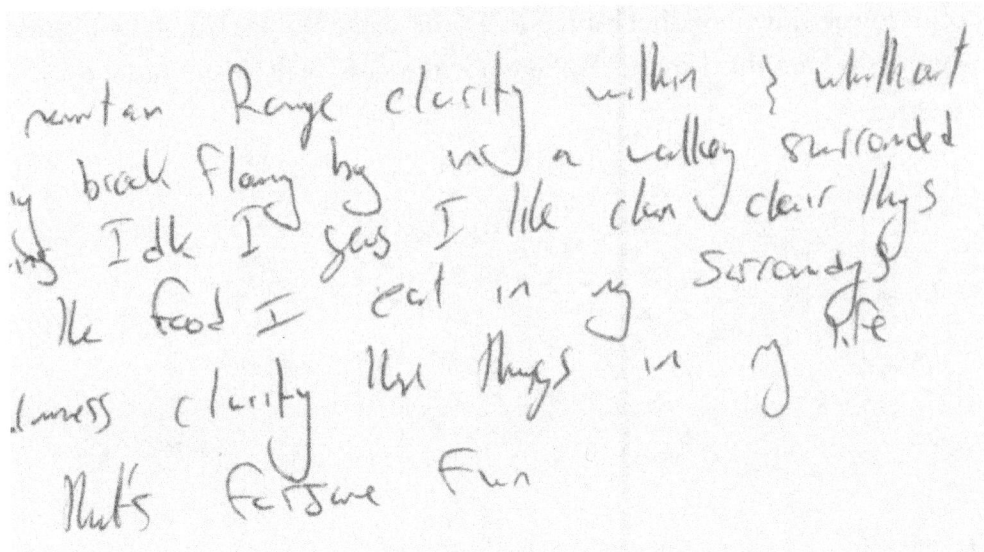

Figure 13-4

Alice's father had wanted her aborted in the third trimester (Figure 13- 5). There was always tension in the family between the parents, and they divorced when Alice was a baby. The father would lash out at Alice on a constant basis, even telling her, "I wanted to abort you." This it's obviously taken its toll on Alice's self-worth and ability to function responsibly. She has no idea how to find her center. She is never content. She uses herself and others as objects and sabotages every positive opportunity that comes her way. Figure 13-5 shows Alice's handwriting at age 19.

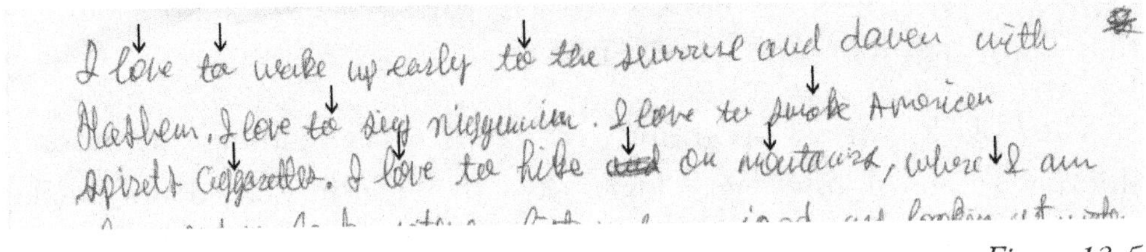

Figure 13-5

Notice that most of her O's are double-looped. *Protect me, help me and hide me.* She writes at the top of the page. *I don't respect anyone who doesn't work hard to earn it.* Notice that the father portion (bottom horizontal line) of her letter I isn't made of much. See her blob cross-outs (covering up mistakes) and roller coaster writing (insecurity in life's direction). She wants to love her father and believes that she must, but her father doesn't reciprocate. She's a girl with a tremendous amount of strength and desire, and a tremendous amount of pain and self-doubt.

Figure 13-6

Wendy, naturally a sweet, friendly, bubbly girl, was abused starting around the age of 10. The abuse greatly affected her. Her positivity was transformed to feelings of being unworthy, dirty, and valueless. Her parents were not aware that any abuse had taken place.

Notice Wendy's handwriting sample (Figure 13-6, Wendy age 24). Her Ys show abuse that took place at a very early age. Her small top margin indicates that she is not comfortable with authority. Her roller coaster writing and the very large spaces between her words show that she feels inadequate and distances herself from people as a defense. The less contact she has with people, the less likely she will be to get hurt.

Observing children's handwriting allows parents and educators to be vigilant. Should signs of abuse present in a child's handwriting, you *must* be compassionate, accepting, and understanding. These children feel isolated, filthy, and unloved. Seek help for them, be there for them, and, above all else, show them that you love them unconditionally.

Notes

Chapter Fourteen

Understanding Is the Key

A 23-year-old boy approached me recently. I'd met him when he was 16 years old. Then, he was a bully who had dropped out of school, not a very pleasant or happy person. When we spoke that initial time and I read his handwriting, he felt I was the first person who ever really "got" him. With everyone always talking about his faults, he'd never felt anyone had ever listened to him. When I told him what I knew about him based on what I saw, he got a chance to understand himself better, and this opened his eyes to the possibility that he could grow and change. Then and there, he dedicated himself to getting his life back together and enrolled in a special school to help him get control of himself.

Even though he was working with a poor self-image from so many years of being down on himself and others being down on him, he worked hard. He stayed in school and is now in a mainstream college. He has a healthy and respectful relationship with his parents and friends, and he is in transition to adulthood, finishing college and looking toward a career and starting his own family.

He learned to control his anger and stop taking out his emotions on others, and he has a strong sense of right and wrong, important and not. He became less defensive, more open. His self-worth has increased, and today he is totally integrated, with no perceivable social issues. He has learned to develop discipline and responsibility, and he knows how to manage his emotions, how to bring himself out of negative feelings and make himself happy. He has fulfilling relationships built on mutual respect and giving, not just bullying. Though he's a little nervous about how he will succeed and what direction his life will take, he feels empowered. He knows he can do it.

It can be extremely difficult to know what's going on in the minds of teenagers, but their handwriting can give us and them a better understanding of what they need and what they're going through. Understanding is the key to encouragement, empowerment, and self-satisfaction. Show your teenagers you understand them. Even if it's only a little bit, it will be sure to breed positive results that can last a lifetime.

Notes

Epilogue: I Wish[9]

---
[9] Source unknown

> "I wish I could say something that would make you trust me," a father once said to his son. Then he continued, "If you give me time, I can prove it to you that I'm worthy of your trust."

A teenage girl and her father were crossing a bridge. The father was scared, so he asked his daughter, "Sweetheart, please hold my hand so that you won't fall into the river."

The teenager said, "No Daddy, you hold my hand."

"What's the difference?" asked the puzzled father.

"There's a big difference," replied the teenager. "If I hold your hand and something happens to me, chances are I may let your hand go. But if you hold onto my hand, I know for sure that, no matter what happens, you will never let my hand go."[9]

In any relationship, the essence of trust is not in its simple joining but in its bonding. Hold the hand of the people you love, and don't always expect them to hold your hand back. Be their lamplighter, even when it's difficult. Your teenager wants to trust that you won't let go.

About the Author

Yaakov Rosenthal is a certified graphologist, life coach, and holistic healer, as well as a trained physiognomist (face reader). He uses these skills during his consultations in high schools and summer camps, where he coaches hundreds of teenagers annually.

Originally from Albany, New York, Yaakov completed his BA in psychology at Hofstra University. He later received accreditation from the Manhattan School of Graphology, where he was mentored by the late Felix Klein, one of the world's most renowned authorities on the subject to this day. Since the beginning of Yaakov's graphology practice in 1992, he has shared his skill on a regular basis with psychologists, guidance counselors, social workers, lawyers, dating services, and Fortune 500 companies. He has given hundreds of lectures on four continents.

Yaakov travels around the country visiting schools as a life coach and consultant and is currently the resident mentor at four high schools in Brooklyn, New York, where he resides with his wife and family.

Appendix A

Twenty Indicators Used to Analyze a Handwriting Sample

1. Space: between letters, words, and lines
2. Margins: top, bottom, left, and right
3. Baseline: where the letters rest on the line that runs across the page
4. Zones: upper (tops of letters like h, b, and f), middle (where all letters reside), and lower (bottoms of letters like y, g, and p)
5. Size of the letters
6. Rhythm: the ebb and flow of the writing
7. Pressure: the force used to write
8. Speed of writing
9. Whether the person writes in print, script, or print-script
10. Connective forms: whether forms are connected by angles or loops
11. Slant direction of letters
12. Line pitch: straightness of the full line of text
13. Fullness or leanness of letters: width or narrowness
14. Cover strokes: retracing portions of letters
15. Initial and terminal strokes of the letter
16. Regularity: fluidity/rigidity (of letters)
17. Capitals
18. The capital letter I
19. Signature
20. Letter formations

Appendix B

Have Your Handwriting Analyzed by Yaakov Rosenthal

Instructions for your writing sample:
1. Use a letter-sized (8.5" x 11") sheet of plain, unlined paper.
2. Write four or five lines about something that makes you happy. Writing can be in cursive, print, or whatever way you normally write.
3. Sign your name with your typical signature.
4. Write two lines as fast as you can about anything you want.
5. On the bottom of the page,
    write your age
    your gender
    an L if you are left-handed or an R if you are right-handed
    your e-mail address
6. Scan the document and e-mail it to info@understandyourteenager. com, or mail the original document to:

Understand Your Teenager
Yaakov Rosenthal
1346 Carroll Street
Brooklyn, New York 11213

You will be e-mailed a 5 minute introductory analysis recorded in a .wav or .mp3 format. Cost 20.00

or

A 20 minute analysis recorded in a .wav or .mp3 format. Cost 49.00

Notes

Notes

Notes

Notes

Notes

Made in the USA
Middletown, DE
29 June 2019